THE NEARLY MEN OF RUGBY LEAGUE

TOM MATHER; GORDON ALLEN

BALBOA.
PRESS
A DIVISION OF HAY HOUSE

Balboa Press books may be ordered through booksellers or by contacting:

Balboa Press
A Division of Hay House
1663 Liberty Drive
Bloomington, IN 47403
www.balboapress.com.au
1 (877) 407-4847

Print information available on the last page.

ISBN: 978-1-5043-1787-0 (sc)
ISBN: 978-1-5043-1788-7 (e)

Balboa Press rev. date: 05/18/2019

CONTENTS

ACKNOWLEDGEMENTS

The idea for this book came from the imagination of Gordon Allen who felt that such a subject needed to be covered for the game of rugby league. As he argued there had been a great many books written about players in the game who had been lucky enough to achieve success in the international arena. Success and failure however are the opposite ends of the same continuum. The failures would never see the light of day while not all those players at the top of the continuum have seen their exploits extolled in print. Neither did they garner the accoladed their efforts deserved from fans.

What about those players who are or were approaching the very top end of that continuum only to be robbed of the highest honour for whatever reason. What of these 'nearly men' those that we could refer to as 'No-Hit-Wonder' players. They were selected for the green and gold, wore the green and gold but because they never did so in a Test match are condemned to mediocrity if such heights can be referred to in those terms. Their stories of success and failure are equally as rich, entertaining and interesting as those who achieve greatness. In some cases, they are even more interesting and poignant.

This book is an attempt to redress the inequalities of such players, they had their moments of glory in the game sadly in many cases all too short. They were however up there with the best of the best and now few if any apart from immediate family actually remember their exploits on the paddock. It is to be hoped this book will put their endeavours back into the public spotlight of the game where they rightfully belong.

When we started to research and write the book, we thought we would be dealing with a rugby league sporting book. While that has been true what we never envisaged was that we would unearth some amazing personal stories, some extraordinarily brave, others tragic to say the least. Two of the players were awarded the second highest military honour for their bravery in World War One. Another with a famous name died in the most tragic and mysterious circumstances.

One player sadly was to pass away while on his way to represent his country on a tour to England. One player fooled the World War One recruitment officers into believing he was old enough to enlist when he was in actual fact just fourteen years old. These and many more fascinating facts are revealed in the book The fourteen stories in the book are a brief account of players back in the days when the game was finding a way forward in both New South Wales and Queensland. At a time when the world was ravaged by not one but two World Wars. The players here actually plied their trade from the earliest origins of the game in 1907 up to the time of conflict in 1939.

We are indebted to Andrew Ferguson for the information he provided with regard to the chapter on David Brown. Equally our thanks go to Paddy McAteer over in Barrow for the information he freely provided to us. To David Middleton for information regarding John Stuntz. To Stuart Quinn for actually identifying Alf Dobbs. We are of course very much indebted to those players whose exploits are recorded here along with all those writers who reported those exploits way back when.

BIBLIOGRAPHY

The following newspapers were used in producing material in the book.

NEW SOUTH WALES

The Arrow, The Cessnock Eagle, The Daily Telegraph, Evening News, Lithgow Mercury, MacLeay Chronicle, Newcastle Morning Herald, Referee, Saturday Referee and Arrow, The Sun, Sunday Times, Sydney Mail, Sydney Morning Herald, Sydney Sportsman.

QUEENSLAND

Brisbane Courier, Bundaberg Mail, Cairns Post, The Daily Mail, The Daily Standard, Darling Downs Gazette, Maryborough Chronicle, Queensland Times, Townsville Daily Bulletin, Truth.

The following books were used in writing this book:-

The Goannas' Legend by Phil Baird

The Rugby Rebellion by Sean Fagan

The Struggle for the Ashes by Robert Gate

A Century of Rugby League 1908 – 2008 by Ian Heads and David Middleton

The Best in the Northern Union by Tom Mather

Rugby League 100 Years in Pictures by Ian Collis and Alan Whiticker

The Encyclopedia of Rugby League Players by Alan Whiticker and Glen Hudson.

INTRODUCTION

It was the American artist Andy Warhol who while in Sweden way back in 1968, fifty years ago now, coined the phrase that:-

'In the future everyone will be world famous for fifteen minutes.'

Nowhere was that quote more apt that in the game of rugby league. The game is littered with players that have seen their career skyrocket virtually in weeks only to nosedive into obscurity equally as quickly.

Equally numerous are those players at whatever level that have come onto the sporting scene and made their debut in this team or that team only to disappear never to be seen again. They are the nearly men, the so called one hit wonders a term that seems more apt to the entertainment industry in general and the recording industry in particular.

Pundits, journalists and fans alike are quick to ridicule the actions of rugby league players who make just one appearance at first grade level, State of Origin or even internationally. To do so is to miss the point for they at least to quote Warhol have had their fifteen minutes of world fame, however small the world. They have basked in the spotlight briefly in their field and no one can take that away from them. Equally as important is the fact that the record books will show their exploits for posterity.

There are sadly some players in the game that never get that fifteen minutes, never experience the bright lights that are the spotlights that go with the fame. They have been selected but have never played, they are in the squad but never received the call to arms at the very highest level. Australian rugby league is littered with such players and players whose standing in the game is at the very highest level. These players had great careers at club level but never received the international call. They went on to have great coaching careers but always on their record was the fact they never had the fifteen minutes of fame all are supposed to experience. While it is true, they played for Australia, but never did so in a Test match. They are what we have referred to as the games No-Hit-Wonders.

This book examines the careers of such players in an attempt to explain just why they were selected but never played. What were their feeling on such occasions, in researching this book it became obvious that many players suffered at the hands of narrow minded and short-sighted selectors and selection policies. It was also apparent that throughout the game there was and still is a 'win at all costs' mentality. Selectors would rather win a Test series three to nil than blood new players into the team to play in a dead rubber Test match.

One must ask the question why take players on tour and yet never give them the opportunity to see if they are up to the standard required for international football. It appears it is very hard for players once in the national side to be dropped however poorly they perform. Equally it must be said that even as a tour is beginning evidence would suggest that selectors had already formulated which team they wish to play in the important games. This attitude from selectors shines through on so many occasions and affected so many players one wonders why it still persists today. That said there was also back in the earlier days the divide between those players from New South Wales and those from Queensland.

Very often there were incidents when a player from the southern state was favoured over a Queenslander when it came to tour and even Test selection. Back in the early days the officials from New South Wales looked upon the game as being theirs and they would do whatever they wanted. After all, it was they that had brought the game to Australia in the first place back in 1907. Whatever the reasons the result remains the same, those players who suffered at their hands were destined to be "No Hit Wonders."

Perhaps the last words on this particular subject should be left to a wise ancient Roman "Cato the Elder" when he stated:-

"After I am dead, I'd rather have people ask why I have no monument than why I have one."

All the players in this book have no monument save that from their families, now perhaps the public knowledge generated by this book of their exploits will be their monument.

CHAPTER ONE

ALF (BULLOCK) DOBBS BALMAIN 1908

There is a saying with regard to greatness that some are born great while others achieve greatness. Then there are those like Alf Dobbs who seemingly had greatness thrust upon them only for it to be cruelly taken away.

Dobbs was born in Sydney on 18th September 1878 and grew up in the Glebe district of the city. He gravitated to the game of rugby union once he left school with first the Glebe club and then Balmain. He quickly established himself as a more than useful player who was equally at home in the rough and tumble of the pack or applying a little guile in the centre.

When news from New Zealand broke back in 1907 that Albert Baskerville was to take a touring party over to England to play Northern Union football Dobbs interest was aroused. Later when it became apparent that Baskerville intended to stop off in Sydney to play a three match Test series against a New South Wales league team, which at that time was still in the embryonic stage Dobbs was hooked. The news broke in Sydney that James Giltinan,

Harry Hoyle and Victor Trumper were to form a league organisation and that rugby union players were being approached to join them.

Giltinan may well not have been the best businessman as his later life proved but he was an entrepreneur of the highest quality. He realised that he needed players and lots of them and the best way to do that was to select as many players as possible to play in the Baskerville Test series. He knew once a player turned out there would be no going back to rugby union and they would have to play the Northern Union game in the League he was proposing to form in 1908. He and Trumper set about the task of getting rugby union players to switch codes and sign to play in the new organisation.

Many players were approached and one of them was the Balmain forward Alf Dobbs. Dobbs had earned the nickname 'Bullock' due to his robust style of play in the scrum and the ruck and when approached he was only too keen to sign on the dotted line. He was attractive to the cause simply because of his versatility being able to perform equally well at prop, hooker or second row, while equally at home playing in the centre.

When Baskerville arrived, Dobbs was selected to play at prop in the second match of the series and so went onto the field to represent New South Wales. It was the only game that he was to take part in but he knew there would be no going back to the union fold. He probably felt it mattered little as at twenty nine years old he was at the back end of his playing career. It did not end well for Dobbs as during the game he hit the back of his head on the ground while making a tackle. The blow was sufficient to cause him to leave the field with concussion and a trip to St Vincent's Hospital following the match. When Baskerville returned to Sydney after a highly successful tour of the old country Dobbs did not figure in any of the three more so called Test games they played. However, with his signing for the new code he could justly be called one of the 'pioneers' of the game.

When 1908 arrived, there was a flurry of activity in Sydney with clubs being formed in many districts. On the 23rd January, 1908, the Balmain Northern Union club came into existence and Dobbs was a member of the new outfit. It is now that things become a little strange not to say weird.

As the inaugural rugby league season began on 20th April 1908, Dobbs is selected to play in first grade against Western Suburbs at Birchgrove Oval. It was a game that Balmain won 24-0 and records show that Dobbs would go on to play in the first five rounds during that season. Then he simply appears to have disappeared from the first-grade scene. We have no idea what happened to him, was he injured, ill or simply disillusioned with the game. Whatever the reasons he missed the last five rounds of the competition.

It seems he made no more club appearances that season but when the party to tour England was announced in the Referee on the 22nd July 1908, while not in the team.

'Hunslet' in the Referee wrote:-

'On the whole the selectors have done their job well those from what I have seen of rugby league football P. Walsh, A. Dobbs, H. Granville, E. Courtney, R. Latta and J. Stuntz would considerably strengthen the party.'

Given Dobbs had not played since round five one wonders just how it was that he figured in the selection thoughts of anyone connected with the game. In truth he did play for the Metropolis against the touring Maori team at The Agricultural Ground on the 17th June, a game the Maori won 29-23. Incredible as it seems he was actually selected to represent NSW against the touring Maori team on Monday the 3rd August. His performance in that match must have been such that when it was decided to increase the tour party to England by the addition of four more players, Dobbs won a place to tour England! Perhaps Giltinan was repaying the faith Dobbs had shown back in 1907 in joining the new code.

Dodds went on that ill-fated tour to England and would figure in only five games. The nearest he got to representing his country came when he was selected to play against the Welsh League as a prop forward at Pendarren Park on 19th January 1909. He was never to come close to playing in a Test match. We see even on this first ever tour the narrow minded and short-sighted selection policy that seemed to have persisted up to the present day. A team mate of Dobbs on that tour was Peter Moir and he also only played in four games on the tour. In a letter home while on tour he gives an insight into the selection policy that seems to have operated on the trip:-

"The team is run by a clique and you are picked by them. I am very disappointed at not getting a game. It is hard as all my people live here and keep asking myself why I am not playing and I cannot tell them a lie."

I wonder if Dobbs was also to suffer a similar fate while in the north of England?

The whole tour was dogged by bad luck, bad selection policies and bad financial management. The Australian players were certainly not up to the standard of Baskervilles players. They also played through one of the worst winters for many years which affected the gates. In the Test matches it would appear players were not picked on performance but at the whim of the so called selection committee. Finally, the gates were badly affected by Giltinans insistence that admission charges for the Australian games be set at one shilling when at the time entry was normally six pence. By the end of the tour the Northern Union was forced to bailout the touring party financially in order that they could return home.

It would appear that his first game on that tour was the fourth one He next seems to have made the team that was to play against York and resulted in a 5-5 draw. Tom McCabe the Englishman in the tour party had been hired by the 'Referee' to write on the tour for the newspaper back in Sydney. The game was the first set back for the tourists and McCabe was not that complimentary about the play of the forwards when he wrote that:-

'Graves has not struck anything like Sydney form; he does not possess the dash he had in Sydney, there being no sting in his play. This remark might apply to a number of forwards.'

It certainly would not have been the start that Alf would have wanted.

He next appears to have made the team for the twelfth game of the tour at Aberdare and this time he was on the winning side by a score of 37-10. It would seem that Dobbs performed much better this time out with the reporter saying:-

'Jones and Dobbs were excellent scrummagers and performed creditably in the loose.'

As the reporter stated the Australian team was an experimental one as just two days earlier the tourists had played a game against Hunslet. So, it was that Dobbs, was for sure on the fringe of team selection.

He had to wait until the Australians persuaded Widnes to travel over to Southport to play them as they had no official game scheduled on New Year's Day and once more, he figured in a high scoring win for the visitors by 55-2. The pitch was not in the best of condition but was playable once the snow had been cleared from the playing surface. Just a couple of weeks later on the 16th January 1909, Dobbs was to take the field in what was for him his biggest occasion on the tour.

The team he was to face was the Welsh League and for the first time Dobbs was in a pack that had real quality, Burdon, McCabe, Dobbs, Abercrombie, Courtney and Walsh. They say cometh the hour cometh the man and so it proved to be in Dobbs case, well until the second period of the game at least. According to McCabe in the Referee he had played very well in the first half and then:-

'Soon after changing ends Dobbs who had been putting in first class work was badly injured and had to retire from the field for the rest of the game. His absence was a big handicap as the Welsh forwards were again in evidence.

Until the time of his forced retirement from the field Dobbs was playing a capital game - was a thorn in the side of the opposing backs and was of great assistance to Halloway behind the pack.

We have no idea just what the injury he sustained was or how serious it turned out to be. Sadly, the match was lost in the last few minutes by a score of 14-12. The Australian team was in a slump losing a good number of games and at such a time Dobbs had put in a great performance only to cruelly suffer an injury that would once again force him out of contention for the big games.

He did not figure in selection until near the end of the tour when once more the tourists went town to Wales, this time to play the Merthyr club. Dobbs was selected to play in the centre for the first time on the tour. Sadly, it was a case of same country same outcome for the unlucky Dobbs. Early in the game he once more suffered an injury. He was off the field for a time in that first half and only to return after the second half commenced and then playing in the full back position. He did not last long and was forced off once more due to the injury and took no further part in proceedings. The Welsh club became the first Welsh side to defeat the tourists winning the game by a two-point margin.

So it was that Dobbs tour was over, when called upon he had not let anyone down but if we are to believe reports the clique would have ensured he was only called on to play when it suited them and form or performance would not come into the reckoning. In one of those ironies that seem to regularly occur in the game Dobbs played as many games on the tour of the 'Old Country' as he had for Balmain during the season that saw him gain selection for the trip.

When the tourists returned home to Australia sadder, wiser and no better off financially perhaps Dobbs felt there was no future for him in the game. He was at that time thirty-one years old and younger players were coming on the scene in ever growing numbers. The records show that he was to play during that 1909 season only one game for the Balmain club. That was against North Sydney and he played in the centre scoring a try in the 24-15 win. In total he played only six games for Balmain in the Northern Union during his whole career. It is probably the shortest career any player has played that won him international recognition.

For whatever reasons Dobbs never played again, he had represented NSW against Baskerville's tourists and also against the Maori touring team. He had then been plucked seemingly from obscurity to go to England with the first ever touring party but never got to represent his country in a Test match. He was just one of those No-Hit-Wonders that lace this great game of rugby league. While he had greatness seemingly thrust upon him by Giltinan in taking him to the north of England with the 'National Team' he never did rise to the dizzy heights of representing his country in a Test match.

Dobbs died in Sydney on 25th June 1954 aged seventy-five.

CHAPTER TWO

JOHN STUNTZ
EASTERN SUBURBS 1909

It is one of those cruel ironies that occur in war that John (Johnno) Stuntz who played on the wing for Australia back in 1907 in that first ever professional rugby match should lose his life in World War One. Ironic simply because his colleague that day playing on the opposite wing for the rival club Frank Cheadle also made the ultimate sacrifice in that same conflict. Stuntz like Cheadle was one of the so called 1907 Pioneers of the Australian game.

John (Johnno) Stuntz was born in Marrickville on 27th June 1885 and growing up graduated to the game of rugby union. In truth at that time it was the only rugby game available to him and any other young boy wanting to play that sport. He was it would seem, blessed with two gifts both useful on the field, speed and cantankerousness! As we shall see he was also a little bit of an enigma in life. He was not the biggest of players when he came into the new game of rugby league being just 5ft. 8ins tall and weighing in at 12 stone, what he lacked in size he more than made up for in heart and aggression.

Stuntz a fast and elusive wingman could never be said to be one who conformed as we shall see, both on and of the rugby paddock and during his short army career. He was born as was said in Sydney in 1885 and first came to sporting prominence in 1906 when he was just twenty-two years old. It was then that he established himself in the Eastern Suburbs Rugby Union Club. He was playing in a first-grade side that included the likes of Lou D'Alpuget, Devereax and the Great Dally Messenger.

It was a club that would go on to dominate the new professional code that was set up in Sydney in 1908. Those years were turbulent times for the Metropolitan Rugby Union who controlled the club rugby in the city for the NSWRU. The players were becoming more and more disillusioned with the treatment they were receiving at the hands of the MRU. Many felt it was they who were generating the cash that was swelling the coffers while they saw none of it.

It was against this backdrop that players noted with interest early in 1907 the proposed tour to the North of England by a professional side from New Zealand. When it became known that those professional players were to stop off in Sydney and that James Gilitinan was proposing that a team of Australians was to oppose them in a three-match series. Stuntz was all in favour of being part of that enterprise. Giltinan had made it clear that following that Test series a professional league was to be set up to play the game under the Northern Union rules. That professional league would commence in the 1908 season.

So Stuntz burned his boats with the amateur code when he ran out onto the Royal Agricultural Ground in the first of the three Tests against the visiting professional All-Black team in front of 20,000 supporters. To be fair it was not his best ever performance but on one occasion he brought the whole crowd roaring to its feet when he collected a pass and getting outside his opposite number he strode away down the wing before turning in field to take the Australians into the New Zealand twenty-five yard area. When the team for the second encounter was announced Stuntz found that his shirt was to be worn by W. Cann and he would watch from the side lines. He would not play again in the series but with the New Zealanders now sailing away to the old country he settled down to preparing for his debut season in the new Rugby League, and what a debut it was.

His Eastern Suburbs club had been formed at a public meeting held in Paddington Town Hall on 24th January. At that meeting well over half of the players who had played the union code the previous season switched allegiance and signed up for the professional code. Giltinan, Hoyle and Trumper had decided that the opening fixtures for the new venture would be played on Easter Monday 1908 and the eight teams in the new league would play two double-headers at Wentworth Park and Birchgrove Park. Eastern Suburbs were to meet Newtown at the latter ground in the first match that would kick-off at 2.00 p.m. The Sydney Morning Herald covered the game which the reporter stated was played at a furious pace and it was a game that would see Stuntz stamp his mark on the game and the sport in a big way, sadly not always for the right reasons.

With the game under way the scoring was initially fairly close and even, then Stuntz took a hand:-

"Frawley, Flegg, Rosenfeld and Stuntz were participants in a fine passing rush. Stuntz getting across the line easily."

It would get better for from a scrum Lou D'Alpuget got the ball and threw out a long pass which missed out the centre and ran straight to Stuntz. Once he had the ball in his hands, he sprinted away from the Newtown cover defence and raced round behind the posts for his second try. The report went on:-

"D'Alpuget, Rosenfeld and Stuntz passed well and once again the fast runner beat all opposition and secured near the posts."

Stuntz had scored a hat-trick and was still not finished as a few minutes later he crossed for his fourth try, it was a record score for a debutant that stood for many many years. With the game wrapped up at 32-16 Eastern Suburbs were coasting having seemingly run Newtown off their feet when we saw another side to Stuntz. The Herald again took up the story:-

"Stuntz and a Newtown player came to blows and Brown separated them. Three onlookers jumped over the fence to come to the aid of the Newtown men and play was stopped until they retired."

On the one hand Stuntz performance with the ball in hand was just what the authorities would have wished for, his antics as the match was coming to its close most certainly would not.

As that first season progressed and Baskervilles' All-Golds return on their way home Stuntz was once more seemingly in favour with the selectors as they selected the team to play the visitors in the first Test. As in the first ever game Stuntz would occupy one wing, Cheadle the other. Both would score a try in an 18-10 win that afternoon and both would retain their place in the second game. Ironically if we believe the newspaper accounts of that second Test it was probably his best game for his country it also proved to be his last! He appeared all over the field in attack making break after break which set up the home side to secure a 13-10 win and clinch the series. Sadly, with the series won and Stuntz playing he thought his best game he was replaced in the final Test.

Whether he was injured or it was simply that the authorities wished to bring in players from Queensland to help the spread of the game we shall never know but he was never to pull on an Australian shirt again. Later in that season when the team that was to tour England was announced Stuntz once more found himself on the outer as his name did not figure in the thirty-four man squad. It was probably a bitter blow for him to swallow but then there is and never has been any sentiment in football. On the other hand, in the lead up to the selection for the tour Stuntz was not playing for his club. The reason for this remains a mystery even today.

When the second season began Stuntz was still with Eastern Suburbs who were not really showing any signs of the glory that was to come just a few short years down the line. Stuntz helped the team to gain fourth spot on the ladder and a place in the Premiership semi-final. In that game they were to meet Balmain who had ended the season in runner-up spot and the form book remained true as Balmain took the spoils by 15-8. In truth it had not been the best of seasons for him but as it came to a close, he had other irons in the fire.

When the Australian tourists had returned home from what proved to be a disastrous tour both on and off the field (The financial side of things would see Giltinan declared bankrupt!!) Five of the tourists had not returned to Australia, they had signed deals with some of the Northern Union clubs in Lancashire and Yorkshire. It was an idea that appealed to Stuntz. At that time players, particularly New Zealanders would simply turn up at a club in England with a letter of recommendation and ask to play trials. Invariably the players secured a contract with the club. It is not clear if John Stuntz did that or if in fact he was approached by someone connected to the Warrington club but as the 1909 season closed Stuntz on 30th September went aboard the 'Suevic' bound for London and from there the northern town of Warrington. It is widely reported that he signed for the club for £125 plus a wage of £3 and five shillings per week.

There is an article in The Referee of the day that actually shed a great deal of light on this area. The Warrington club were in fact very keen to sign Dally Messenger and had begun negotiations to bring the great centre over to Wilderspool. At the last minute when all seemed settled a problem arose and Messenger did not sign the contract. The Warrington officials who were keen to get an Aussie star asked rugby experts in Sydney for the name(s) of a suitable replacement. The name all the experts came up with was 'Johnno' Stuntz and as his team mate Dan Frawley was already with the club, they brought over Stuntz. The pair played on the flank with Frawley occupying the wing spot and Stuntz playing centre to him, and very successful the pairing turned out to be!

However, in typical Stuntz style he caused controversy even before he arrived in England. The evidence suggests that he had actually promised two clubs that he would play for them. Along with Warrington the Barrow club expected him to play for them. When he set sail for England, he did so with his team mate Dave Brown who was to play for Barrow. ***(See a later chapter on Dave Brown.)***

We know that five Australian players who went on the tour in 1908, actually stayed in England and signed for clubs over there. Stuntz was one of the first if not the first Australian to actually find a club while in Australia. He was also lucky in as much as just ten days after he set sail the Northern Union declared an international transfer ban. This was to stop Australia and New Zealand losing its top players to the 'Old Country', the very thing Stuntz was doing. He may or may not have known it but he was joining a club that already had one of the premier wingmen in the game albeit one who was approaching the end of his career in Jack Fish. Fish would play 321 games for the club in his career and score 251 tries a record which would stand until overtaken by the legendary Brian Bevan.

It is hard to believe such facts would bother Stuntz in any way and in the only season he was with Warrington he showed just why the club wanted him. On his arrival he was quickly fitted into the first-grade squad and on the 4th December 1909, around two weeks or so after his arrival he pulled on the primrose and blue shirt for the first time. In total he would play nineteen games for the club and score thirteen tries, it was a strike rate that even today is worthy of any wingman. It was a season which saw him assist the club to seventh spot on the ladder and more importantly take them to the very brink of a Challenge Cup Final. In the first round of the cup Warrington had defeated Wigan Highfield by 31-3 to set up a second-round tie also at home to Millom. The Cumbrian side was easily disposed of 37-0 and a sterner test awaited in the next round. The great Hunslet side came and they too would leave on the wrong side of a 7-0 score line.

In all probability Stuntz played his last match for the club on 2nd April 1910, in the cup semi-final against Leeds. The game was played at the home of Broughton Rangers, Wheater's Field and Warrington and Stuntz came so very close to a final appearance being pipped at the post by Leeds 11-10. The game over Stuntz stay in England also came to its close and he returned home and to the Australian game this time not with Eastern Suburbs but with South Sydney for the 1911 season. Ironically in the two years he would remain with Souths his former club would win the Premiership twice.

In 1912, Stuntz changed his life around somewhat as first he enlisted as a fireman 4th class and was based at the Headquarters. Having done so he then proceeded to marry Celia the love of his life. He very quickly rose through the ranks in the fire service and in that same year following his marriage he was stationed at Kogarah where he and Celia settled into married life. By June 1914 he had been promoted to the rank of 1st Class fireman.

As the 1913 season began Stuntz had moved yet again this time to Western Suburbs he would play for the club for two more seasons. Now working as a fireman for the Sydney Fire Service he had no reason to enlist particularly given his occupation and marital status when war was declared. He however enlisted on 3rd March 1916 and was allocated to the 14th Reinforcements for the 17th Battalion. With his basic training completed first at Cootamunda camp and then Liverpool Private Stuntz set sail for England and the war on the Western Front. Sadly, it was not to be all plain sailing for him. You may well be able to be somewhat of a larrikin in civilian life but once in military service such behaviour is not tolerated in the same way as he would find out to his cost. The Wiltshire with him on board left Sydney on 22nd August and we can see from his service record that on 18th September he was charged with being absent without leave. It appears he failed to turn up for parade and was sentenced to 24 hours detention and seven days field punishment No 2. (This meant he was manacled and shacked whilst he was going about his daily routine.)

Once the Wiltshire docked in England, he and his colleagues were sent to complete their training at Bovington Camp in Woolwich and it was there he would once again fall foul of military discipline. He was charged with being absent without leave when he failed to return to camp by midnight on 24 October, he had only been in the country since the 13th October! He was found and arrested at 9.30p.m. the following evening and when brought up before the Commanding Officer was ordered to forfeit one day's pay and confined to camp for one day. It is hard to understand just why he did such things as he was not new to a disciplined routine. He had been a serving officer in the fire service where such things were a pre-requisite and he had risen quickly through the ranks. Also, his service record shows that prior to enlisting he had served a one year spell with the Royal Australian Garrison Artillery so knew military life and discipline.

Whilst these two offences in themselves were not that serious or considered to be serious by the Australian military his third offence was quite the opposite. Once more he would absent himself without leave but this time having left the camp and missed roll call at 0.800 hours on 2nd of December 1917, he was not found or did not return to camp until 12.00 hours on 24th January 1917! He had been absent for a total of fifty-three days. Just why he absconded and where he went we do not know. The question is after only seven weeks in England had he met up with people in the south of the country that he knew and perhaps stayed with them. A more likely explanation is that he would go to somewhere that he knew and to see people or relatives that he knew and such a place could only have been at Warrington the town where he had previously played rugby.

When he returned to camp, he was punished by ten days confined to camp and 28 days loss of pay. This punishment does seem to be quite lenient given the length of time he was missing from camp but could be explained by the desperate demand for men on the front line at the time. This was later to be increased so that in total he would forfeit 82 days' pay which in the end amounted to around 20% of the days he was actually in the army. Luckily for him he was not charged with the more serious offence of desertion as that would have carried a prison sentence. The sentence would have been even longer had he been on or near the Western Front. If he had been serving in the British forces there was every possibility he could well have been charged with desertion and if found guilty could have been shot at dawn! Thankfully the Australian authorities took a more humane approach to these matters.

Once back in camp and with his sentence served by the middle of February 1917, he was along with the rest of his colleagues dispatched to Europe in readiness for the coming spring and summer offensives that the High Command were planning. He arrived at Etaples and following further training was finally marched in to join the 17th Battalion who were stationed on the Somme. They had suffered a harsh winter in the Somme trenches and so when Stuntz arrived the weather would have been much kinder but an offensive was already being planned for the Battalion. It was an offensive that became known as the Second Battle of Bullecourt.

The war was finally if somewhat slowly turning in favour of the Allies and the Germans had actually pulled back to new positions that were considered to be pretty much impregnable, the so called Hindenburg Line. The French were proposing to launch an attack on the new positions and the 17th Battalion were to be involved in a supporting attack at Bullecourt to the north of the French offensive. That offensive had failed but it was decided to continue with the attack at Bullecourt and so it was that at around 3.45a.m. the Aussies went over the top to follow a creeping barrage from their own guns designed to protect them before they actually attacked the much vaunted Hindenburg Line. It was in truth the first time Stuntz had actually gone over the top or seen action of any kind, sadly it proved to be his last.

At the end of that first day, 3rd May 1917, when incredible as it may seem the Aussies actually breached the Hindenburg Line but lacking support were forced to retreat. At roll call Stuntz was not present to answer his name. After preliminary investigations on the front he was posted as 'Missing in Action.' It would be some weeks before any further action was taken in his regard but once the dust settled so to speak evidence began to be gathered in preparation for a Board of Enquiry that would be held to ascertain the position with regard to Stuntz. This was normal in every case when a soldier was posted as missing. The first requirement really was to establish if the soldier was alive or dead. If he was alive what evidence was there that he was now a prisoner of war or had he been shipped back to England for treatment to his wounds etc.

As evidence was obtained from various soldiers involved in the assault on that first day it must be appreciated that during the course of that second conflict at Bullecourt Australian killed and wounded totalled some 7482. Stuntz was just one of many and as the evidence was slowly acquired it quickly became apparent that confusion had reigned on that day. Private W.D. Pilgrim stated on the day Stuntz died that:-

"...the Battalion was in action at Bullecourt. They hopped over the top at about 4.00a.m. sometime between 8 and 11 a.m. informant saw Stuntz lying dead near the German wire at their objective. It was quite evident he had been killed outright. Informant and Private Crowe (killed later that day) put Stuntz in a shell hole and left him there. The objectives were not gained that day and our men had to retire."

It has to be remembered that Pilgrim was giving a statement to an officer in February 1919, almost two years after the event but was certain that Stuntz was dead. This was different to what he stated in June 1917, when questioned because then he was of the opinion that Stuntz had been badly wounded and they were unable to reach him to bring him back to their own lines. He went on to say ***"he was very bad indeed when I saw him and was not expected to live."***

More evidence was taken in September 1917, from Lance Corporal B. Galway who told officers :-

"Lance Corporal Davis of 'A' Company told me he had seen Stuntz killed in an attack at Bullecourt. We at first held the ground taken but were driven out by a counter attack, so that his body was left out in front."

Both soldiers were sure that Stuntz was dead whether by shell shrapnel or gun fire was unclear and his body never recovered. That confusion was cleared up somewhat by Private T. W. Brown who stated that Stuntz had been killed by shell fire at Bullecourt and his body never recovered. If the enquiry thought they had reached a stage where they could arrive at a conclusion they were sadly mistaken for a short time later in October 1917, Private E.W. Hubbard added to the confusion:-

"I saw him on the morning of May 3rd 1917 near the German wire. This was after the attack was broken and we were taking cover waiting the opportunity to go back. I saw Stuntz running about from shell hole to shell hole with only his pants and shirt on. I think he was off his head. The shelling was very heavy at the time."

The problem facing the Board of Enquiry was a simple one, was Stuntz dead or alive. In truth the manner in which he met his end was not really the issue whether he died from shell fire or gun fire the result was the same. In the end they concluded that Private John Stuntz had been 'Killed in Action' on the 3rd May 1917, and that his body was not recovered and was unlikely ever to be found.

A post script to this was that after the war a request to the German High Command with regard to Stuntz resulted in a statement that they had no trace of Private Stuntz. He lies to this day probably close to where he fell on the battlefield almost one hundred years ago.

Stuntz had been looked on as one of the future stars the game would be built on back in those pioneering days of 1908. He had the new game at his feet and had pulled on the shirt to face Baskerville's men but that was for New South Wales. Back then it could be argued that as this was the only state playing the game, he was gaining international recognition. Sadly, that was not to be the case as it was only much later in 2004 that the authorities decided such games as those and the occasion, he opposed the visiting Maori team in 1909 would be recognised as Test matches and players awarded Kangaroo status. During his lifetime and for sadly much longer John Stuntz was destined seemingly to be just one more player deemed a 'No Hit Wonder'.

Private John Stuntz died on the 3rd May 1917, aged just thirty-one. Sadly, like thousands of Diggers has no known grave and is commemorated at Villers-Bretonneux Memorial.

CHAPTER THREE

DAVID JOSEPH BROWN EASTERN SUBURBS 1909

In 2004 the Australian Board of Control that has responsibility for all things international connected with the Australian game met. At that meeting the decision was made to award Test status to the games between Australia and the touring Maori way back in 1909. In doing so they set a conundrum for many historians in so much as one of the players involved in one of those Test matches was David Brown from the Eastern Suburbs club. Nothing remarkable in that you may well think until you realise that he became the third David Brown to play a Test for Australia. To add further confusion all three players played for the Eastern Suburbs club prior to gaining Test status.

The player we are concerned with was the Brown who was the first to play for Easts back in 1908 when the club was formed. To say that his life was something of an enigma would be an understatement as we shall see. His life on the field was clouded in uncertainty whilst his life off the field was without doubt one of mystery and possible intrigue. Most certainly it was colourful.

He was born in Sydney on the 13th May, 1886 the fifth son of George and Brenda and grew up in and around the Eastern Suburbs. He along with a number of young men who turned out to become greats in the game of Northern Union football first plied their trade in the only rugby played at that time the union code. He went along to the Eastern Suburbs rugby union club and by 1906 was playing alongside such players as Dally Messenger, Devereax, Breckenreg, the D'Alpuget brothers, John Stunts and Albert Rosenfeldt. He and they would have remained there had not the new code arrived from England via New Zealand and Albert Baskerville.

In 1907, when it was known that professional rugby was coming to Sydney, he along with a number of his team mates took the offer made to them by James Giltinan to switch codes and play against Baskerville's All Golds. He had to wait until the third of those Test matches before he was to get onto the paddock. On the 24th August, 1907, at the Royal Agricultural Show Ground he was to play in the centre. The three-quarter line that afternoon was Cheadle, Messenger, Brown and Devereax, three Easts players and a Newtown player.

When the new year came in and a meeting was called at Paddington Town Hall with a view to forming an Eastern Suburbs Northern Union club Brown was eager to attend. In truth he had little option as he like all who had played for Giltinan's team were banned from the rugby union. That meeting on the 24th January did form the new club and he like the other players got down to serious training for the up-coming new season.

The season kicked off on Easter Monday and Brown played in the centre of the Easts' side against Newtown. He had a quiet game barely getting a mention in match reports which were dominated by the four try performance of John Stuntz. He did get on the score sheet early in the second half when he crossed for a try. It was late in the game which was won by Easts 32-16 that he got a second mention and then only because when Stuntz and a Newtown player got into a 'blue' it was Brown who stepped in and separated the players. He also pulled Stuntz away from a number of supporters who had invaded the field and were heading straight for the wingman.

In that first season he played eleven games missing only one game. The club actually qualified for the finals and in the semi-final, they were to play North Sydney. They won as they say going away by 23-10 and so went into their first Grand Final. Their opponents a fortnight later were arch rivals South Sydney. In an absolute cracker of a game Souths just took the honours winning 14-12. In truth they deserved the win as they scored four tries to Easts two. In addition, Brown had actually played in the tour trial game Giltinan had organised as he prepared for his ill-fated tour to England. It seemed like all was going very well for the young Brown who was just twenty-two with the rugby league world at his feet.

At this point it may well prove beneficial to the reader to examine just what was happening off the field for Brown or what we think was happening. He was living in the Eastern Suburbs at this time and the place was not the suburb it is today. On the contrary it was at the time a place of sly grog shops and prostitution was rife. There were also a number of embryotic 'razor gangs' in the district. It was in this environment that we see Brown who was a Roman Catholic is living with a woman to whom he is not married by the name of Olive De Loitte. That in itself was a situation that would be frowned upon by a great many folks. To add insult to injury not only that but he was also the allegedly the father of two children by the lady. Ena was born in 1907 when Brown was just twenty-one years old and Laurence in 1908.

Just how was he supporting his family, certainly the money he was earning from playing the game would not be sufficient. We know from later evidence which will be examined in more detail that his mother was to refer to her son as ***"a troubled boy"***. Just what is meant by this we perhaps will never know. We can speculate that given the area he was living in away from the game, he was mixing with the wrong people. Whatever he was doing he seems to have provided some sort of support for his family by whatever means.

There is a suggestion and it must be stressed that it is just a suggestion that he was mixing with the wrong people off the paddock. On the field he was playing with some great players as we have seen and so would or should that be, could not fail to impress. He was a player equally at home playing five-eighth as he was on the wing or in the centre. As the second season came around, he was still holding down a place in the first grade and played in nine games for the club. Having missed the first game of the season he was an ever present for the rest of the season.

The reason he missed the first game could well be because on the 10th April 1909 he and Olive De Loitte were married. Perhaps he had decided to make an honest woman of Olive, on the other hand it could well have been because she was carrying his or more precisely her third child. The fact that Olive had been happy to live as it were 'in sin' with him for so long adds a little to the suggestion that she could well have been working in the Eastern Suburbs as a prostitute. Once again it must be stressed that no evidence could be found other than the circumstantial one stated above. However, she did at times go by the surname of De Loitte or Croker or Brown and why would she do that?

As the season was coming to a close, we see Brown take yet another turn in his life. There is a brief article in the Referee on the 22nd September which reported that:-

"D. Brown received offers from Warrington and Barrow and will make the trip with his club mate to play for Barrow."

His club mate was none other than the wing man John Stuntz. He and Stuntz boarded the Mooltan and sailed from Sydney on Saturday 25th September. Evidence from England would suggest that Brown had written to both clubs and in his letter may well have exaggerated somewhat about his playing ability. He would have stated that he had played for Australia which was true but he had not confided that the game was not one of Test match status. Both Warrington and Barrow would have assumed that it was and so were keen to sign an Australian international player. Throughout this whole period, it appears that both Brown and Stuntz were close friends and maybe one encouraged the other to go over to England. It could be speculated that Stuntz insisted that Warrington offer terms to Brown as a condition of him joining the club.

Certainly, when the Barrow club were informed that Brown was on his way they were delighted. He would become the first overseas player to sign for Barrow in their history. Both the club and the newspapers in the north of England made a big event of the signing. What Brown had no idea of was that he was leaving a team of great players in a fledgling league to play for a club of no stars in the Northern Union. He had barely two seasons experience in the game and was just twenty-three years of age. He would be up against players with ten or more years, experience in the game and who were battle hardened. Equally the game played in England would have differed greatly to that he was used to playing for Eastern Suburbs. Sadly, his endeavours were doomed to failure.

So, it proved to be the case. He arrived at Barrow to a big fanfare of publicity as was to be expected as the first overseas player to come to the club. The club found him employment at the Vickers Shipyard in the town. Barrow was a far cry from Sydney and without doubt he would have had difficulty understanding the local dialect. I wonder just what he made of local folks greeting him with the phrase 'Hey do marra' rather than g'day mate!

While in the shipyard he actually played a game in order that the club directors could get their first sight of his ability. He played for the Engine side of the Yard against the Ship Side of the Yard. There was no doubt he was a marked man as all wanted to take a crack at him but he held his own and showed that he had speed, a good body swerve and was a hard tackler. He was then selected to play on the 27th November 1909, against Runcorn in the home game. This was his first game in the Northern Union and he failed to impress the local reporter that is for sure. Writing in the Barrow Herald 'REFEREE' had this to say:-

"What on earth is the use of bringing David Brown over from Australia. All he did was stand still and catch cold. I am anxious to see him on attack, never had the ball in hand to gauge him. He played centre but would be better at half back. I cannot recall him receiving one pass."

In fairness to him he must have performed reasonably well for after that game on the Tuesday evening at training (the 30th November) he signed a contract with the club. On the following Saturday when the team travelled to play Broughton Rangers, he actually made a fifty yard break that resulted in a try for the team. Sadly, it all went downhill after that and the off-field antics in Sydney seem to have been continued in Barrow. Back then however off field indiscretions tended not to make the newspapers as reporters had no desire to blacken any players character. Sadly, we shall never know the real story of his life in Barrow as the back issues of the local newspaper The Barrow Herald were stored in a basement. Many years ago, that basement flooded and did irreparable damage to the material stored there so no record now exists.

It was his performances on the field that began to cause reporters some concern. Certainly, the standard of his play was not what was expected of an international player. The reporters began to dig around and could come up with no information that informed them of Brown's international status. There is a photograph of Brown in an Australian shirt wearing a cap. On close examination the date on the cap in 1909 which would fit in with him playing against the Maori that same year. The clamour grew that perhaps he was a charlatan and had duped the Barrow club. As the season progressed it became obvious that his performances on the field were adding little to the team effort. Given his on and off field actions it appeared that after just eleven games the club dropped him and he was not to play first-grade again.

When the 1909-10 season came to a close Brown once again boarded a ship this time bound for home. When he arrived home in the middle of June 1910, he would have received something of a shock, for greeting him when he got home was a pregnant Olive who was carrying her fourth child which as we shall see must have been conceived some time toward the end of March when Brown was still in Barrow. He does seem to have accepted the situation which adds more to the belief as to just what his wife was doing to support the family while he was away.

On his return he once again returned to the Eastern Suburbs club and actually played one game. That was on the 30th July just a month or so after he arrived home and the opposition was Newtown. The game ended in a 4-4 draw and that was the last time he was to play a first-grade game. Interestingly he played at five-eight that afternoon and his half back partner was Barney Dalton. Nothing remarkable in that you may imagine until you know that Dalton was a known member of a Sydney razor gang!

(Dalton was an outstanding footballer for the Eastern Suburbs club and actually won two Permierships with the club. When he finished playing the game, he became a member of the notorious Kate Leigh razor gang that were involved in the Sydney gang wars in the 1920s. On the 9th November 1929 outside the Strand Hotel which was on the corner of Crown and William Street in the city he was shot dead by Frank Green.)

Sadly, his life was destined to take a turn for the worst in the most dreadful way. On his return he had secured a job on the railway and was working at Homebush Station (Now at Olympic Park.) His duties involved him in tending to the signal lights which at the time were lamps fuelled by oil. On Christmas Eve he went to work as he had been doing for some months. At 5.30 in the afternoon he was found on the side of the track where he had been attending to the signal lights suffering from multiple injuries. The Sydney Morning Herald carried the following article in their edition on Boxing Day:-

"David Brown a railway porter at Homebush Station, was found about half past five on Saturday against the home signals in an unconscious condition and suffering from shocking injuries to the head and body. He was attended to by a local doctor and subsequently removed to Prince Alfred Hospital by the Civil Ambulance, but died shortly after admission. It is thought that Brown who had charge of the signal lamps was knocked down by a passing train."

The question must be asked what was he doing to the lamps prior to that time surely, they did not need to be lit as this was the middle of summer and in broad daylight. The Daily Telegraph on that same Boxing Day carried a report which gave more details as to his injuries:-

"David Brown a prominent footballer was fatally injured on Saturday night while about to light some lamps at the signals. Just after 5-30

he was found against one of the home signals bleeding from wounds all over his body. It is believed that he had been knocked down by a train. He was taken to the Royal Prince Alfred Hospital by the Civil Ambulance suffering from compound fracture of the left thigh, compound fracture of the left arm and severe lacerations about his body and head."

Surely in broad daylight had he been hit by a train the driver would undoubtably have seen him on the track or working on the lights as he approached him. Equally mysterious was why was he not missed by his work mates, or at just what time had he been struck by a train. The question must be asked did he fall or jump, that we shall never know. Also, consideration should be given to the company he kept and the view that he may well have been pushed. Certainly, the inquest held on the 13th January 1911, shed no light on any of these questions and the report into the accident for some reason is incredibly short and uninformative. It read:-

"I find that the said David Joseph Brown at the Royal Prince Alfred Hospital on the 24th day of December 1910 died from the effects of injuries accidentally received on the same day through being run over by a railway train at Homebush Railway Station."

It seems incomprehensible today that such an accident should receive a scant examination by a Coroner who also did not order an autopsy. I know times were different back in 1910, but surely an accident of such a nature particularly on the railway was worth a more thorough examination. No one seems to have been questioned not even the driver of the train that supposedly hit Brown. Also, the Coroner had no idea and seemed uninterested in just when the train struck him.

It was assumed I supposed that Brown was not drunk at the time of the accident as the Coroner's report stated **"No intemperance"**. As I said times were different back then but surely there were many questions that should have been asked and addressed by the Coroner that sadly were not and cannot be asked now. Who found him and at what time, how many trains had passed him during the time he was missing. If a train had passed him surely that driver would have seen him and stopped the train to report the incident. These are questions being asked now that should have been asked way back in 1911.

Brown was buried on Tuesday the 27th December and was interred at Waverley Cemetery. Just a week after his death his wife Olive gave birth to her fourth child. This fact as was stated earlier clearly shows Brown was not the father of her fourth child.

Throughout his short life Brown who was just twenty-four when he died, was never afforded the privilege of being a Test player and therefore must be deemed to have been yet another 'No-Hit-Wonder' in this great game of rugby league. It was not until 2004 when the Australian Board awarded Test status to the game Brown played against the Maori.

CHAPTER FOUR

STAN CARPENTER NEWCASTLE (1909)

Contrary to popular belief the Newcastle rugby league pioneer Stanley Franzien Carpenter was not born in the northern coal city of Newcastle but rather in Woolloomooloo, in the heart of Sydney on 22nd September 1885. His family, he had an elder brother Leslie and a sister Lily, then moved up to Newcastle while he was still a youngster.

As a youngster he grew into a big strong young man whose strength and power had been developed by working in the coal mines in Newcastle. He had also spent time working as a labourer on the railway at nearby Dungog.

When he moved through the ranks of the Central Newcastle rugby union club at 5 foot ten inches and around twelve stone, he was the ideal build for a forward. He quickly developed a reputation locally as a hooker or prop of some considerable skill and ability. He had also developed into a more than useful goal kicker. We should not be surprised by that as he seems to have followed into the footsteps of his elder brother Les. Les had served in the Light Horse Regiment in South Africa during the Boer War. On his return he had continued with his rugby career.

In 1906 at the age of twenty-one he married local girl Jean McDonald and settled down into married life little knowing that the sporting world had other things in store for him. He was like many rugby union players at that time growing more and more disillusioned with those running the game. It seemed that there was one rule for the players with regard to professionalism and another for the officials. Players often received no expenses or a bare minimum, often just three shillings a day when playing for their club or a representative side. Officials on the other hand were able to wine and dine themselves without affecting their so called amateur status.

Since the advent of the professionalism of the Northern Union as it was deemed over in England in 1895, Australian officials seemed to have adopted the same attitude toward professionalism and the league game as their English counterparts. The draconian restrictions placed on players via rules on professionalism stifled any leeway when players were injured. That was bad enough but what rubbed salt in the wounds for many was as was stated the fact the rules did not apply to officials running the game.

All of this discontent had been brought to a head in Australia when Albert Baskerville revealed he had decided to take a team from New Zealand to play the Northern Union teams over in England. While travelling to England in 1907 Baskerville had been persuaded to stop off in Sydney to play a three-match series against players James Giltinan, Victor Trumper and Harry Hoyle were busy signing up to their new Rugby League. With the series completed and the Kiwis away in England work had begun in

Sydney in preparation for the new professional league to begin in the 1908 season.

In an effort to spread the game out to a wider New South Wales audience Harold Hoyle and the Secretary of the league James Giltinan travelled up from Sydney to Newcastle in an effort to get players to switch codes in that city. Initially their efforts fell on deaf ears and then the rugby union officials appeared to shoot themselves in the foot. They dropped the great Pat Walsh from a representative side and many in Newcastle saw the decision as being political as he was in some way perceived to be connected with the growing professional game. The disillusion many players were feeling increased and at the instigation of a group of players and officials Hoyle and Giltinan paid a return visit. This time their efforts were better rewarded and a number of players decided that they would be better off playing the new code.

One of the players in that formation group was the Central Newcastle hooker Stan Carpenter. On the 10 February 1908, at Pike's Rooms on Bolton Street the proposition was put forward to form a Northern Union club and break away from the constraints of the rugby union authorities. Unfortunately, there was not enough support and the move failed. However, when news of the meeting became public knowledge a number of those players who attended the meeting were isolated by the rugby union authorities. They like their counterparts in England deemed simply meeting with people connected to the professional code was enough to taint them. Hoyle and Giltinan travelled up to Newcastle in secret one more time and held a meeting at the Tattersall's Hotel on Hunter Street.

Following that meeting it is reputed that fifteen players met outside the Central Hotel in the city and there they agreed to form the Newcastle Rugby League club. That was on the 10th April, 1908, and legend has it that all the players signed their names on the back of an opened-up cigarette packet. At that meeting by unanimous consent Carpenter was elected captain of the newly formed club. Carpenter was ably assisted in those early days by William "Jerry" Bailey a free scoring wingman in the union game. That done they set about learning all they could about the rules of the new code. Not an easy task as there were no Northern Union rule books in the whole of Australia at that time. The New Zealand tourists in England at the time actually brought back with them a good number of rule books to be distributed throughout the clubs in the newly formed league.

As the initial season began a Newcastle club was to play in the new league. On the opening day of the initial season the 20th April Newcastle were to travel down to Sydney to meet Glebe at Wentworth Park. Glebe at that time were thought to be the best club in the new league. The reason behind the thinking was that Glebe were coached at that time by probably the most knowledgeable player of the new code in Australia in Englishman Tom McCabe. McCabe had moved to Sydney from the great Wigan club around 1906 and when Baskerville brought over his touring team McCabe was probably the only person in the country with personal experience of playing Northern Union football.

The Englishman had been busy teaching Sydneysiders the rules of the new code visiting all the clubs initially at the behest of Giltinan. There he had held coaching and training sessions with the players. The All-Gold players on their return from England had actually spread themselves out so that all the new clubs were visited by a number of New Zealand players who spent time coaching the clubs in the rules and tactics of Northern Union football.

Carpenter had been selected as captain of the Newcastle outfit and he and they acquitted themselves very well just losing to the Glebe club 8-5 in that first match played on Easter Monday. The reporter for the Referee writing of the game stated that Carpenter was prominent throughout the game. Carpenter had developed into an excellent hooker who could also kick goals a precious commodity. He also had an eye for a gap and quickly established a reputation as a scorer of tries as well. All involved would have been pleased with the performance in that first ever game for the Newcastle club.

Just two days later he was selected in a Newcastle representative side to play the returning All-Gold tourists. If that were not enough, just three days later still he actually ran out to face the All-Golds yet again but this time representing the Northern Districts. His reputation as a hooker or prop forward of skill and scoring ability was growing in the new game. It appeared that his good form continued throughout the season at club level and brought him to the attention of the likes of Giltinan and the other selectors based in Sydney. At the season's end he was the Newcastle club's top scorer with two tries and sixteen goals for a total of thirty-eight points.

During that first season the Newcastle club steadily improved and more than held their own against the Sydney sides. Of the nine games played in the league the newly formed club won four and finished a respectable fifth on the ladder. As the season was coming to a close James Gilitinan was planning a venture that was to have a profound effect on the new game. Sadly, it was to also profoundly affect his personal life as well.

Following the great success of Baskerville's tour to the old country Giltinan decided to follow suit and take a touring squad over to England. To that end a trial game was organised and the Probables were to meet the Possibles. When the tour party was selected following the game Stan Carpenter was in the squad and looked upon as the second-choice hooker. It was then fate took a hand for Carpenter had suffered a broken leg and was forced to withdraw from the tour squad. One wonders just what direction his life may have taken had he gone on that ill-fated visit. Five of those players on the tour remained in England signing for various clubs in the Northern Union. Carpenter at just twenty-three years of age with his reputation and abilities would have undoubtedly attracted the attention of many English clubs.

The following season the club continued to improve and they would actually finish up in third spot on the ladder and so made their first finals series. They played South Sydney in the semi-final and sadly were on the wrong side of a 20-0 score line. Carpenter however continued to show the form that earned him representative honours the previous year. There was one game that perhaps would have pleased him for than most while playing for his home town Newcastle. That came on Wednesday the 16th June 1909. On that afternoon Newcastle took on the touring New Zealand team. What made that special was that Stan would captain the Newcastle team while playing in the second row, more importantly he was to pack down in front of his elder brother Les. Sadly, the game was lost by a score of 3-6 but according to reports Stan was 'prominent' throughout the game.

It was not to be the only representative game he was involved in that season. In this area he was unwittingly to be involved in perhaps one of the bitterest and longest running disputes in the history of the game. Before that he was to gain representative honours against the touring New Zealand Maori. On the 24th July that year, 1909, Carpenter took to the field at the Agricultural Ground in Sydney in the sky-blue jersey of NSW to face the Maori thirteen. In a match that excited the supporters and reporters alike the visitors came out on top winning 24-21 in front of 20,000 supporters. "Hunslet" writing in the Referee following the game thought that 'Davies, Sturridge and Carpenter were fair' in their performance in the game. The following Wednesday the two teams faced each other again and once more the visitors were victorious again, this time by 14-11. On this occasion Carpenter played in the second row for NSW such was his versatility.

He must have done enough in both of those game for when the selectors met following the second game to select an Australian side to play the Maori in a "Test"

Carpenter was selected. Once again, he was to occupy one of the second-row berths in the game, sadly he was for the third time to be on the losing side going down 16-14. From the point of view of this book why then is he actually in the no-hit-wonders category? The simple answer is that it was not until much later that the game's authorities were to actually give Test status to the games against the Maori in 1909. So, for all of his life while a kangaroo, he was not considered to be an Australian Test player.

There were to be two other games that season that would cement Carpenter's reputation as a player of note. The first came in his home town of Newcastle on Wednesday 4th August, Newcastle were to play the touring Maori side. Up to that time the Maori were undefeated on the tour and in truth few if any gave the home side much chance of winning the match. It seems Carpenter and his team mates had other ideas.

When the whistle blew to start proceedings, it was the red and white striped shirts of the home side that launched wave after wave of attacks on the Maori line. When the visitors did get the ball, they met with fierce defence which restricted any progress. Then the home side were awarded a penalty and Carpenter stepped up and slotted over a magnificent goal to give his side a two point lead. Just a little later in the half after yet another attack Carpenter was tackled just inches short of the line. It was all the Maori could be to keep their line intact.

It got better for Newcastle as from a scrum in the Maori twenty five yard area Carpenter won a quick ball and Padfield picking up simply left the defence flat footed and crossed for a three pointer. Carpenter once again stepped up and tacked on the two extra points and against all expectations the home side led 7-0. That was the score line as the half time interval came and all in the ground expected that the Maori would overcome the locals in the second forty minutes.

While it was true that the second stanza saw the visitors attack with greater frequency the Newcastle defence stood firm. Asher got clear and thrilled the crowd by carrying out his trade mark flying leap over a would be tackler, in this case Walsh but he was caught short of the line. The efforts of the Newcastle forwards were taking their toll and the Maori began to win more and more of the scrums. As the half progressed and the score line remained unchanged the visitors began to get frustrated and play became a good deal rougher with punches thrown. Late in the half the Maori backline managed to get clear and Taunui managed to breach the home line for an unconverted try. With the end of the match fast approaching the visitors had an opportunity to win the game when Wikiriwhi scored but the goal was missed.

When the whistle blew it was Carpenter and his men who had lowered the Maori colours for the first time winning the game 7-6. While the players were delighted with the win, they had little time to celebrate or even savour the victory. The reason for that was that come Saturday they were to play South Sydney in the final game of the regular season. Souths like the Maori were unbeaten during the regular season and once again few if any felt the home side could win the game. Surely the efforts of Wednesdays game would catch up with them on the Saturday.

What ever the feelings were some three thousand turned up to watch the game and they were not disappointed. The Newcastle players carried on where they had left off on Wednesday and launched attacks at the Souths line. In a fast, open game, the Souths players responded in kind and the crowd was constantly on their feet cheering attack and defence by their favourites. It was Newcastle who took the lead with an unconverted try. The score remained unchanged until Cox collected a clearing kick on the Souths twenty five yard line. Instead of launching an attack he cleverly called for a mark and handed the ball to the skipper Carpenter who kicked the resulting goal to take the lead out to 5-0.

That was were the scoring came to an end and strive as they may no side could again trouble the score board attendant. When the game ended the Newcastle players walked off the field with a second victory in four days. What those two victories did was firstly generate a greater interest in the new game of Northern Union rugby league in Newcastle. Secondly it caused the folks in Sydney to look on the coal mining city as a rugby area that was not to be under estimated in future. Thirdly it let the rugby fraternity see that Carpenter was a player of quality and equally important a leader of players on the field.

With the second season coming to a close as was said he was to be involved in a game that led ultimately to the bitterest and longest running controversy in the game's history. During the 1909 season in a concerted effort to increase the playing strength throughout the game a bold plan had been hatched. The players in the rugby union the so called, Wallabies who had toured England in 1908 were secretly approached and efforts made to persuade them to switch allegiance to the new rugby league code.

Flegg and Larkin the League Secretary secretly met with players and eventually were successful in getting a good number to switch codes. The problem was that the players had got wind of the fact they were being approached individually and decided to negotiate terms collectively. Instead of paying them a fee for each of the matches they played in as had been the original plan the league was forced to pay each player quite a considerable sum of money to give up their amateur status. The cost of getting the players to switch codes was so high that the league approached the then President James Joynton-Smith to foot the bill. This he agreed to do provided that the league undertook to repay the loan. In order to fund this, it was decided that a three-match series would be arranged between the Wallabies and the Kangaroos.

The games would be between existing league players, the Kangaroos and rugby union players from the England tour the Wallabies. The three games duly went ahead under league rules and surprisingly the Wallabies won two games to one. The league players wanted an opportunity to square the series and asked for a fourth game to be arranged. As the attendance at the previous three meetings had not raised enough revenue to totally repay Joynton-Smith the league agreed and scheduled the fourth game at the Agricultural Ground on the same day as the Grand Final between South Sydney and Balmain was to be played.

When the event was announced the Grand Final was scheduled to be played first before the fourth 'Test'. Balmain objected strongly to that feeling the final was being demeaned. Also, they objected to being part of a plan to raise revenue for Joynton-Smith. The Balmain club refused to play the final and claimed that South Sydney would also be boycotting the game in protest. Sadly, the South Sydney club back then and ever since denied that claim and on the day, they turned up and took to the field, kicked off and thus claiming the Premiership by default. The claims and counterclaims of both clubs still rattle around the game to this day.

Following the 'none' game the main game took place when the Wallabies and the Kangaroos took to the field. Stan Carpenter was wearing the hooker's shirt that afternoon and helped the league players level the series by winning the game 8-6. There is little doubt that the events of that afternoon did little to enhance the game as a whole in the short term as the Grand Final debacle tainted the game then and even to this day. On the other hand, a good number of quality players had switched allegiance at a time when the league needed such players. For Carpenter it was the end of a very good season for him and sadly the end of his and the Newcastle club's participation in the Sydney competition.

In Newcastle the league authorities were of the opinion that the area was strong enough to run its own competition and set about organising their competition to run in the 1910 season. Consequently, the Newcastle club withdrew from the Sydney competition That first season provided the very highest of thrills for Carpenter but also took him to the very depth of despair off the field. Sadly, on the 30th March of that year his young wife suddenly passed away and he was left a widower at the age of just twenty-four. Jean was just twenty three years old when she died. On the rugby field however the first ever tour by the English was under way and an England team was to play a game up in Newcastle.

The game was to be played on the same day as the first ever Test between the two countries in Australia was to be staged in Sydney. For the Newcastle game all those Englishmen not required for the Test were sent to play in Newcastle. Due to injuries there were only eight available and so five Australian players were drafted in to cover this, Frawley, Devereux, Morton, Byrne and Burge taking to the field to represent the 'Old Country'. Not for the first time in a representative game Carpenter was on the wrong side of a 24-8 score line.

The following Wednesday the two teams were to meet for a second time with the English putting out a much stronger team lead by skipper James Lomas. The score ended up at 40-20 to the visitors but Carpenter must have been delighted that his team had put twenty points on the touring team. What would have pleased him even more was that he managed to get his name on the score sheet after converting one of his sides tries.

In the domestic game Carpenter had joined the South Newcastle club and skippered them to a Premiership. He would later switch allegiance to the Newcastle East outfit and also guide them to a Premiership. Sadly, war clouds were gathering in Europe with alarming speed in the middle of 1914. When war was declared between England and Germany Australia promptly also entered the conflict. Carpenter as we shall see was no stranger to military conflict and just two weeks after war was declared went into a recruitment office in Randwick and re-joined the army. The widowed twenty-nine year old was welcomed by the army with open arms.

When he enlisted, on his service records he revealed that he had spent over two years serving in the Australian Artillery Forces at the turn of the century. Not only that he had served a six-month spell in Natal, South Africa, as part of the forces fighting in the Boar War. (***A search of the service records was unable to unearth just what his service in South Africa entailed. It must also be noted that this war was not a conscript war and those who went to fight did so as volunteers. In all probability Stan would have travelled down to South Africa at the same time as his brother Les who also served in the Boer War. We know this from his obituary when he died in 1939. At the funeral of Les his coffin was draped with the Union Jack in recognition of his service in that war. However again a search of the war records failed to unearth the record for Les Carpenter.***

The Australian War Memorial Research Centre did throw a little more light on the situation. They informed us that some Australians went to South Africa under their own steam and once there served with the British Regiments already in the country. That being the case he was offered the rank of corporal on enlistment but declined and preferred to enter the forces as a mere private. He was assigned to the infantry 2nd Battalion, 1st Division. Once he arrived in Egypt to continue his training he transferred to the Medical Corps as a stretcher bearer.

He like many other Diggers were in training for the upcoming action at the Dardanelles due to occur in April 1915. On that fateful day the 25th April Carpenter complete with stretcher was in the third wave of troops that landed onto the chaos that was the Gallipoli beach. There is little doubt that he and his mates in the Medical Corps were kept very busy on that next twenty-four hours. However, with the invasion around thirty hours or so old Carpenter and his mate Edward Roberts were making their way along the beach mindful of the sniper fire they were constantly subjected to as were their colleagues.

What happened next was described by Charles Bean in his official history of the conflict. According to Bean It was late in the afternoon when a New Zealand soldier Lance-Corporal Ross was looking at the abandoned landing craft on the beach through his powerful viewfinder. He noticed a sailor in what appeared to be a life-like position amongst the dead soldiers. He thought nothing of it until a while later when he again looked and saw that the sailor had actually moved so obviously was still alive. To his astonishment the sailor began to crawl away from the landing craft and began to hobble towards the beach. That was the signal for Turkish snipers to open fire on the man.

Ross took four men and went out to try to rescue the man but soon came under intense fire themselves. They were forced to take cover but did work along the beach until they were within shouting distance of the wounded man. They called to him and he crawled slowly toward the rescuers and they were able to bring him to safety. He told his rescuers that there had been eight wounded soldiers in the landing craft but four had since died but four were still alive and needed rescuing.

It is worth stating Bean's own words as to what happened next:-

"The remaining survivors appear to have been rescued by stretcher bearers of the 2nd Battalion. From his position on Walker's Ridge Lieutenant Westbrook of this Battalion had noticed like Ross some movement from one of the figures before Fisherman's Hut. He asked two stretcher bearers of his Battalion by the name of Carpenter and Roberts if they would try to bring this man in. The two men went at once, taking their stretcher. As they neared the boats fire was opened up on them. They found several of the men still alive, and made the journey four times each time bringing in a wounded man.

Some New Zealanders then went out with an improvised stretcher to pick up a fifth, but the task of carrying him on the makeshift bed was almost impossible. The two Australians with their stretcher therefore went out again and helped them to finish the journey."

All the time Carpenter was under constant fire from Turkish snipers as well as shell fire but that did not deter him. His brave actions were observed by Lieutenant-Colonel Braund who was a serving member of the NSW State Parliament. For his brave actions Carpenter was actually recommended by Bean and Braund for a Victoria Cross the highest honour in the British Army. Sadly, the request was turned down by the Australian High Command so the recommendation never went forward to the British High Command.

The Battalion did set about the task of officially mentioning Carpenter in dispatches. Their description of events while less flowery than Beans is most enlightening about Carpenter:-

"These two stretcher bearers on 26th April went along the beach under heavy fire to rescue wounded men of other units who had been lying in a stranded boat near the 'Fisherman's Hut' for over thirty hours. All the occupants of the boat had been killed or wounded by machine gun or shrapnel fire. The stretcher bearers rescued four wounded men although under fire while going to the boat taking the wounded men out and returning."

While it adds nothing to Bean's account it is what is written in the previous recommendations column of the report in his service record that shed light on the character of Carpenter. It appears this was not the first or last occasion that he came to the attention of his superior officers.

The official record tells us that acts of gallantry were observed and recorded by Lieutenant-Colonel Braund KG on the 25th April 1915. Once again on 19th July 1915 by the late Lieutenant-Colonel E.S. Brown and yet again on the 15th November 1915, this time by Lieutenant-Colonel Cass CMG. What this tells us is that Carpenter was carrying out his duties as a stretcher bearer with great courage, while under enemy fire over a long period of the Gallipoli offensive.

The reasons for the recommendation of the Victoria Cross not being pursued can only be speculated upon after all this time but there was then and is now the view that the decision was a political one. The British High Command already had on its desk six recommendations for the Victoria Cross to soldiers from the Lancashire Fusiliers for brave actions during the landings on the morning of the 25th April. Now they had a similar recommendation for a colonial soldier. I suppose the British High Command would be reluctant to consider such a recommendation for an Australian soldier as they had little if any notion of how the Australian Army conducted itself on the battlefield. A more likely reason could be that at the time the Victoria Cross was only awarded to commissioned officers and Carpenter was an NCO! The reader must draw their own conclusions but Carpenter was not awarded the medal. It is strange is it not, that we now are all familiar with Simpson and his donkey and how he went out into no-man's-land to bring back wounded men. Just how many of us are aware of Carpenter and his bravery.

The powers that be however did recognise the bravery of Carpenter on that day and on another occasion and he was eventually awarded the Distinguished Conduct Medal. This is second only to the Victoria Cross with regard to gallantry and was awarded to NCOs. Carpenter would receive his medal on the 19th August 1916 by no less a military man than General Birdwood for a further act of bravery this time on the Western Front.

With the withdrawal by the Allied forces from Gallipoli later in 1915 Carpenter found himself removed from the frying pan only to be dropped into the fire on the Western Front at Pozieries. In July 1916, at the Battle of Pozieries Carpenter once again found himself in the spotlight. The attack by the Diggers had not met with success and the stretch between the two trench lines, the so-called No-Man's-Land was littered with Australian dead and wounded. Over a four-day period while once again under enemy sniper and shell fire Carpenter went out into the No-Man's-Land time after time to bring back wounded Diggers. There can be no doubt his actions saved countless lives over those four days.

His courage was thankfully this time acknowledged by both the Australian and British High Command. He was recommended for the award of the Victoria Cross. It was the first "official" recommendation from the Australian Army authorities for such an award during World War One. Sadly, once more for whatever reason it was turned down. It has to be said that to carry out one great act of bravery as he had done at Gallipoli is one thing but to carry out a second in similar circumstances is unbelievable. At Gallipoli he perhaps had little knowledge or time to think of what danger he was facing but at Pozieries he would have clearly understood the dangers he faced. He faced those dangers and his own fears not once but many times in that four-day period during his excursions into No-Man's-Land. Each time he went out he returned with a wounded soldier. We have no idea how many owed their lives to his brave actions but his commanders were well aware of his efforts.

The official mention in despatches by the 2nd Battalion on 1st August 1916 read:-

"At Pozieries France during period 22nd/25 July. This N.C.O. throughout the operation showed remarkable gallantry under the most trying conditions and although the shelling was almost unprecedented in severity nothing seemed to daunt the matchless courage of this N.C.O. Time after time he went out into 'No Man's Land' to collect and tend wounded. There is no doubt that it was through his efforts that so few of our Battalion wounded are missing. Officers and men are unanimous in their expression of admiration of him."

Across the bottom of the citation in his service record is written the words Recommended for the Victoria Cross. There were also written statements from Captain H.G. Yeoman and Captain R.S. Henderson attesting to the courageous efforts Carpenter made during those four days of the battle.

For these great acts of sustained courage at Gallipoli and on the Western Front he was eventually to receive the Distinguished Conduct Medal. The citation read:-

"His Majesty the King has been graciously pleased to approve the award of the Distinguished Conduct Medal to the under mentioned None Commissioned Officer for acts of gallantry and devotion to duty in the field.

No 607 Corporal Stanley Franzien Carpenter.

For conspicuous bravery during protracted operations under heavy shell fire. Time after time he went into 'No-Man's-Land to collect and tend wounded, and it was owing to his fine courage that so few of his Battalion's wounded were missing."

Given the modest nature of Carpenter he would go on to be awarded that Military Cross which he received on the orders of General Birdwood on the 19th August 1916. His service record (page 34) confirmed this but it appears he never collected that. He was awarded other medals at the end of the war as was every surviving soldier and these would have been posted out to him. We can assume the Military Cross did not reach him simply because after his death in 1962 his second wife Olla actually applied to the authorities in a letter in April,1967, for his medal to be sent to her.

With the war over Carpenter returned to Newcastle and despite his age returned to the game and continued to promote rugby league in the northern city. Sadly, having survived the war tragedy struck him much closer to home. Having completed his army service, he returned home to Australia. Unfortunately, prior to his arrival home, in 1919 it was a country like many others in the world ravaged by a deadly strain of flu often referred to as 'Spanish Flu.' It struck many families and Stan Carpenter was not exempt as his sister Lily was to contract the flu and sadly passed away on the 11th April 1919.

He married for a second time in 1920 to Olla Stokes. Sadly, tragedy had not finished with the brave man. Having moved to Kempsey he ran a Wine bar and Billiards saloon in the town. He once again began playing the game and represented Northern Districts at the age of forty-three. He retired from the game but continued to coach the game at various levels. Unfortunately, family tragedy had not yet finished with Stan. Sadly in

1933 on 13th June, his young son also named Stanley while riding on his bicycle home from school for his lunch he was hit by a car and died he was just two days past his eleventh birthday.

The MacLeay Chronicle on the 14th June carried a brief account of the accident:-

'At 12.50pm on Tuesday Master Stanley Carpenter only son of Mr and Mrs Stanley Carpenter of Smith Street, rode a bicycle down Herborn's Lane onto the bridge approach at East Kempsey and came into collision with a Ford car driven by Mr Fred Harvey of Gladstone. The lad sustained a broken left leg, below the knee, a pierced left lung and a fractured skull. Dr Rankine hurried the lad to the District Hospital where he passed away about eight o'clock that evening. The bicycle was completely wreaked, and the radiator of the car smashed, showing the impact was of considerable force. Much sympathy is felt for Mr and Mrs Carpenter in their sad bereavement.'

Stan had survived the fighting overseas in World War One only to suffer great personal losses in his own family at home.

After that Carpenter slowly withdrew from all sporting activities and settled into a quiet life with his second wife. Carpenter died on 31st May 1962 at the age of seventy-seven and was buried at Sandgate Cemetery in Newcastle. He was in all probability the second most decorated Digger from that war. In 1918, Leslie Thomas Axford was awarded the Victoria Cross. Carpenter was and still is one of the most highly decorated Australian Rugby League player along with Joe Murray ***(See a later chapter for Joe Murray's exploits)*** and yet now his brave exploits have been lost in the mists of time.

For the whole of his life sadly, he was never given the status of being an Australian Rugby league Test player. The authorities did not afford Test status to games against the Maori tourists of 1909 until 2004 long after he had died and his exploits had been long forgotten. For that reason and that reason alone Stan Carpenter lived his life out as a 'No Hit Wonder.'

CHAPTER FIVE

ARCHIBALD THOMAS HARVEY BUNDEBERG 1909

Maryborough is a lovely little town on the Mary River mouth in Queensland. It is situated some 255 kilometres north of the Queensland capital Brisbane. In truth its main claim to fame would come from being the birth place of Helen Lyndon Goff who entered this world in 1899. Who on earth is Miss Goff you may well ask, she is better know worldwide by the name she used when she emigrated to London. Once there she became P. L. Travers and wrote the eight Mary Poppins books.

Another Maryborough native born eleven years earlier was Archibald Thomas Harvey. His arrival into this world was announced in the Maryborough Chronicle of the 22 March 1888 two days after his birth. The announcement read:-

"Harvey at her residence John Street the wife of H. M. Harvey of a son."

Little did any one know at the time just what this young man was to achieve in the sporting world. As he was growing up there were a number of games he could play, cricket in the summer and rugby union or Aussie rules in the winter. It was the former that was to attract him to it.

By the time he reached the age of nineteen all sorts of upheavals were occurring within the game but they were mainly affecting the game in New

South Wales. He read in the newspapers of a New Zealand professional team who were travelling to England stopping off in Sydney to play a series of matches but it bothered him little where he was living. That all changed in February of 1908 down in Brisbane.

A number of rugby union players in the city would meet up every lunch time at the 'Courier Mail Corner' and discuss all manner of things. What was occupying their conversation one day was the progress the Northern Union game was making down in Sydney. One of the players Sinan 'Siney' Boland decided to do more than just talk. Legend has it that he wrote a number of letters to other players and after borrowing five pence mailed off the letters.

The gist of the letters was the proposal that the players should get together and emulate the actions of Giltinan and form a Northern Union league or what Boland termed the Queensland Rugby Association. To that end a meeting was held at the Railway Hotel in Brisbane on the 28th February ***(ironically that was the same day that Albert Baskerville and his 'All-Gold' tourists set sail from London aboard the Mongolia bound for Australia and then home)*** where the new rugby body came into existence. Their first order of business was to publicise the new body and its aims which they did through the newspapers. The rugby union authorities as had those in Sydney were appalled and began banning anyone involved with the new body.

Arrangements were made in secret to bring Baskervilles squad up to Queensland to play a series of matches and it was those encounters that cemented the game in the State of Queensland. The new body then played a three match series down in Sydney against New South Wales and although they were defeated in all three games four of the northern state players were then selected for Giltinan's tour over to England. Plans then were firmed up for a league similar to that in Sydney to be established in Brisbane to commence in the 1909 season.

As these events were being enacted Arch Harvey then just twenty years of age decided that while the rugby union game he played was something he enjoyed the new faster and more open northern rules game seemed to be more suited to him. Evidence suggests that he was actually playing for the Natives team up in Bundaberg in 1908. The Bundaberg Mail of 1st June that year carried a match report between Natives and Woongarra in which it stated that:-

"The kick at goal was entrusted to Arch. Harvey who made no mistake, and from a somewhat difficult angle landed a beautiful goal."

For whatever reason he made the decision that it was the new code that he would play and he joined the exodus of players leaving the rugby union ranks. He left the up country rugby union game to try his luck in the new code down in Brisbane. He settled on the newly formed Fortitude Valley Diehards club in which to throw in his lot.

The new code was subject to poor coverage from the newspapers that had after all been covering the union code for many, many years. Not only that but the new game was ridiculed at any and every opportunity by the media. The new league persevered and four clubs entered the new competition Valley, Toombul, North Brisbane and South Brisbane which began on the 8th May, 1909. The young Harvey did not gain a spot in the first-grade side until three weeks later when he made his debut against South Brisbane in round four.

Arch was a big strapping lad equally at home in the front row as he was in the second. He proved to be a more than useful player in the scrummage and scrum work but the open spaces allowed him to use his pace to better effect than had been the case in the old game. He did have speed to burn for such a big man and put it to very good use in the Valley side. His Valley club defeated South Brisbane by nine points to seven and it was his try that helped to seal the victory. The report in the Brisbane Telegraph suggests it did not take Harvey long to make his mark on the game:-

"Valleys were first to score and this they did soon after the game commenced. Harvey emerged triumphant from a sort of rough and tumble near the goal posts."

In that inaugural season he went on to play five games and helped the club to secure the first ever premiership title. With the season ending the authorities were preparing for the representative season to commence.

On the 12th June a trial match was arranged in order to select a team to represent Queensland in a game against New Zealand on the following Saturday. There is a report of that game which incidentally Harvey did not appear in. The same report however, went on to say that the selectors had named the team and strange as it may seem Harvey was selected to play in the second row. The whole squad were to report for training on the following Tuesday, Wednesday and Thursday evenings.

The match took place at the Cricket Ground on Saturday 19th June and there were over four thousand there to watch the encounter. It is interesting to note that the referee was J. Fehilly who was one of the three selectors of the Queensland side! The visiting New Zealanders won the match by a score of 40-25. The two team were to meet once more on the up coming Wednesday. Once again it was the visitors who took the spoils 27-19 but Harvey was not selected for the Queensland side for whatever reason. On the Saturday the Australian and New Zealand teams met in a Test match which sadly Harvey watched from the side lines.

Following the Test matches the Queensland team travelled to Sydney for an interstate game and Harvey once more did not figure in the proceedings. Records show that he seems to have stopped playing for the Valley club at this time for some reason that can only be speculated upon at this time. What is very interesting and shows once again that there is nothing new in the game of rugby league was an interstate club match. On Wednesday the 21st July a match was played at the Exhibition Ground between Newtown who were billed as the Sydney Premiers and the Valley club who were billed as the Brisbane Premiers. Once again Harvey's name is missing from the Valley line up.

The New Zealand Maori touring squad were about to travel up to Queensland to play a series of matches against the state side and following that a team representing Australia. The Queensland officials once more organised a trial match in order to select a team to oppose the Maori. The match was staged at the Brisbane Cricket Ground on Saturday 31st July between the 'First Thirteen' and the 'Second Thirteen'. Harvey was selected to play in the second row in the first thirteen side. Having not appeared on the paddock for the best part of a month we can only assume he had been injured.

The match was a little one sided with Harvey and his team mates winning easily enough by 27-16 and he maintained his try scoring reputation crossing the whitewash for one three-pointer during the game. Following the game, the selectors sat down and selected the thirteen to represent the state against the Maori and Arch Harvey at just twenty one years old was to pull on the maroon jersey for the second time playing in the second row.

The game was played in front of around 7,000 supporters at the Cricket Ground in perfect conditions. The game was hard and fast with both sides attacking at every opportunity it was from such an attack that the first score in the game came. As the match report tells us:-

"Then as the outcome of a mighty rush by the home men, Harvey scrambled through and obtained the first score of the match amidst the greatest enthusiasm."

Arch had maintained his record of scoring tries and in the process helped the "Maroons" to defeat the Maori by a score of 21-11. Following the game, the selectors met once more to select the team that would meet the visitors on the coming Wednesday. Whilst a number of changes were made, some positional, Harvey retained the second row spot for the next encounter. In a game that was equally as fast and exciting for the watching crowd this time it was the visitors who came out on top. They over turned a 17-12 deficit to win the game by a score of 36-28. Harvey however maintained his scoring record once again crossing for a try in the second period.

Following the game J, Fihelly who was to be the sole selector for the Australian team to meet the Maori on the Saturday decided on the team he felt could win that game. On Saturday 14th August the Australian team that took to the field in the maroon and sky-blue jersey was:-

McGregor, Stuntz, W.Heidke, Woodhead, O'Brien, Patfield, H. Heidke, Brackenreg, Anderson, Nicholson, Ross, Harvey, Buckley.

When the game commenced it proved to be as fast and furious as the two encounters with Queensland had been. The Maori attacked from the kick-off and after a few minutes scored a converted try to take the lead 5-0. With both sides then attacking at every opportunity the crowd was constantly on its feet roaring on the Australian team. They levelled the scores when the second row Nicholson cleverly ran in for the try which Brackenreg converted to get the extra two.

The Maori once again took the game to the home team and a second converted try soon followed and the lead was once again five points at 10-5. It was the home side that then took the game by the scruff of the neck when first Harvey picked up and used his speed to break clear and score. Just a few minutes later the winger John Stuntz repeated the feat and once clear scored in the corner both tries were unconverted. The upshot was that at half time the Australians led 10-11.

The second period saw both sides adopt a more cautious approach neither wanting to lose the match. The home side were to score yet another converted try to stretch the lead to 10-16. The only other score came from an unconverted Maori try to make the final score 13-16. The interesting thing is that Harvey had maintained his incredible record for scoring a try on debut. This time he had scored while representing Australia rather than his home state of Queensland.

It has to be said that coverage of the game in Queensland by the press was pretty sparse and far greater prominence was afforded to the old code of rugby union when it came to the reporters. For that reason, the description of the game and Harveys contribution is very brief in the Brisbane Telegraph. It is even briefer in the Referee down in Sydney simply because the game was played in Brisbane. The two teams were to meet again on the following Saturday in Sydney at the Agricultural Ground unfortunately for whatever reasons Harvey was dropped from the side.

At this point in the story the details are at best sketchy and at worst non-existent with regard to his career and life. He seems to have literally dropped off the radar. Certainly, he did not play another game for the Fortitude Valley club, if he did it is not recorded. The following season he did not figure in the inter-state games for Queensland or against the England team that toured in that 1910 season. The same is true for the 1911 season again he gained no representative honours. It seems inconceivable that a player of his obvious talents would not be on the radar of at least the Queensland selectors if not the national selectors based in Sydney. The question must be asked was a simple explanation that he had suffered a career ending injury!

The next time we see him is in 1915 when he is living and working as a clerk down in Melbourne. The war was some eight months old and just after his twenty seventh birthday on the last day of March he was to enter a recruitment office in the city and enlist. He had on his attestation form stated that he had served sixteen months with the State Cadets and for five months been an N.C.O. at the depot. Given this information when he enlisted the authorities sent him to the Sixth Officer Training School. On the tenth of April 1916 he was given the rank of Lieutenant and assigned to the 14th Battalion, 4th Infantry Brigade.

On completing his training, he was then shipped off to France and the Western Front and served there the whole time he saw active service. That services was destined not to be that long. He arrived at the front around the first week of June and the Brigade were stationed at La Rolanderie near to Armentieres having arrived from defending the Suez Canal. Soon after his arrival in the front line he was to see action that sadly would be his first and also his last. It was an action that was mentioned in despatches and occurred on the night of the 2nd July 1916 just a couple of weeks after his arrival. Just what occurred is perhaps best described by his Commanding Officer and recorded in his service record.

"The Corps Commander wishes to express his appreciation of the gallant conduct of all who took part in the raid on the enemy trenches on the night of 2nd/3rd July carried out by a party consisting of 6 officers and about 83 other ranks of the 2nd Australian Infantry Brigade.

A brief summary of the events is given below:-

The party encountered a hostile patrol (strength 10 or 12) in No-Man's-Land at the moment when our main bombardment was commencing, this party was forced back into the zone of our fire and all of them were killed. Great difficulty was experienced in crossing the enemy's fire. Our scouts and some of the wounded threw themselves on the wire and formed a bridge for the assaulting party to cross. The enemy's trench was entered in spite of fierce opposition and severe casualties were inflicted. One of the officers of the raiding party was

Lieutenant Archibald Thomas Harvey

What we know is that Harvey was wounded in that assault being shot in the thigh and the abdomen. Whether he received his wounds on the approach to the enemy trench or while fighting in the trench is not clear. What is clear is that the wound to the abdomen was very serious and he was quickly shipped to a field station for treatment when his men got him back to their own lines. From there he was shipped over to England for hospital treatment and recuperation. Luckily or perhaps unluckily depending upon your point of view his injuries proved not to be life threatening but they were of such a nature that he was invalided out of the army and returned to Australia.

Like his rugby league career his military career was relatively short and while successful we would never know if he could have gained higher honours. On his return home he continued with his life and lived to the age of seventy passing away on the 12th May 1958. Throughout his life he was never afforded Test status for the game he played back in 1909 and so for that reason should be considered to be a No-Hit Wonder like so many others in the game.

In a cruel irony that so often occurs in this world his son John was not to be as lucky as his father. In the conflict that was World War 2 John sadly was shot and killed in Papua New Guinea at Lae Ping in 1943!

CHAPTER SIX

SIDNEY JAMES FENNELLY NORTH BRISBANE? 1909

The game of rugby league began in Sydney in 1908 some one hundred and ten years or so ago. In that time the game has thrown up more than its fair share of mysteries. None more so than that of one player who went through life as a no-hit-wonder and yet in today's world he actually won two Test caps. Such is the mystery surrounding this player that even the spelling of his name if in fact it really was his legal surname is confusing. Reporters way back then could not make up their minds if his surname was Feneley, Fennelly, Fineley or Fenelly. Even more intriguing is that there is little or no record of him playing for the North Brisbane club, he is officially associated with in the Queensland records yet he rose to the very pinnacle of the game.

However, we are getting ahead of ourselves, so let us start at the very beginning. The records within the game tell us that Sidney James Fennelly ***(I will use the official correct spelling of his name or the name he used)*** was born on 22nd March 1887 in Newtown. If you search the records you will not find an entry for his birth. The reason being that he was actually born Sidney James Leonard. The name of his father is unrecorded but his mother was in fact Mary Leonard. We can however make a reasoned assumption that his father was Edward John Fennelly.

The reason for this is a simple one, just three years later in 1890, Mary and Edward were married and a good number of off-spring followed. First came Lily born in 1891 while the family were in Goulburn. Then came Edward Reginald in 1895, Thomas in 1897, Mary in 1901, Walter in 1902, Michael in 1903, and finally Kathleen in 1906. The question is simply was Sidney actually legally adopted once his parents married or more likely, did he just use the family name?

So, he was one of seven siblings and growing up he tended to get involved in a number of sports. As a youngster he was noted for the speed in which he travelled over the ground so became a sprinter of note. His second love without a doubt was cricket where he excelled as a batsman and as we shall see played at the highest level. In the winter with no cricket or athletics to occupy him he turned to rugby union. There is little record of his early life in Sydney and we do know that he first come on the radar when he moves up to Queensland and begins playing for the Mount Morgan rugby union club. It was not the only use he made of his speed.

The evidence suggests that he was at that time also using his considerable ability as a sprinter to advantage. He was travelling about North Queensland appearing anywhere that professional sprint races were being held. He invariably ran using an assumed name and more often than not he ran away with the prize money. Many years later when his wife divorced him, she revealed that when they married in 1909, he was a professional sprinter under contract to a Frank Collingwood. It could well have been that Collingwood recognizing the talent the young Fennelly possessed signed him up and moved up to the north of Queensland.

As was the norm at that period country fairs that towns held would hold sprint races with a cash prize. The young Fennelly would have been paid a weekly wage by Collingwood and they would travel around to compete in such races. The problem came when Fennelly began winning with monotonous regularity. In such cases his handicap would be greatly reduced thus affecting his chances of winning. To counteract this, he and Collingwood began to enter events using an assumed name and even altering his appearance by letting his hair grow or grow a moustache and beard.

There is evidence of this in a letter in the Darling Downs Gazette on the 21st May 1908, when the Secretary of the Southbrook Sports Club D. G. O'Shea wrote:-

"I am instructed by my committee to ask you to publish the disqualification of Sidney Williams otherwise S. J. Fennelly for fraudulent entry in the Southbrook grand handicap 130 yard race on 2nd April 1908."

In the same little piece O'Shea informs us that Fennelly had won £55 on New Year's Day in an event at Bundaberg and also £4 on St Patrick's Day. That was a considerable sum of money back in those times. So, we can see that by attempting to disguise Fennelly was quite profitable for both himself and Collingwood.

This charade came to something of a head in February 1909 when at the age of twenty two he was banned by the Mount Morgan rugby union club over his professional running activities. The newspaper reported of his appeal against the life ban imposed on him.

Having failed in that appeal to be reinstated it seems that he was forced to take whatever work he could get but in that same year 1909, on 6th April he married Margaret Ann Steward and settled into what turned out to be a stormy relationship that was destined not to last over long as we shall see later. On the day he married he took his new bride back to her parent's house and left her to go training so was still entering sprint races. Also being banned from rugby union his attention turned to the new sport of Northern Union football and once again we see him to quote Winston Churchill become a riddle inside a mystery wrapped in an enigma. It seems he did play the game but finding evidence that identified which club he played for proved very difficult.

They say that as one door closes another opens, and for Fennelly that proved to be the case. Being banned from rugby union he suddenly found that down in Brisbane a new code that of the Northern Union was providing him with an opportunity to carry on playing rugby. As we know the game began in 1909, and on the 8th May of that year the four inaugural clubs

North Brisbane, South Brisbane, Toombul and Valley played the first ever round of fixtures. If you examine the Queensland records for the game or even the Australian player records both show that Fennelly played for the North Brisbane outfit.

When you examine the match reports in the Brisbane newspapers of these games, they list the teams representing each club. On that first Saturday Fennelly did not figure in the North Brisbane team that took to the field. Neither did he figure on the team sheet for any of the other three clubs. It was the same on round two, three and four so just where was he? It gets even more confusing because on the weekend of 12th June there were no league games played. The reason for this was that the authorities had arranged a trial match aimed at selecting a Queensland side to meet the touring New Zealand team the following Saturday at the Brisbane Cricket Ground.

On the 14th June the Telegraph carried a match report of the so called Possibles versus Probables game. Strange as it seems Fennelly was not in either team on that afternoon. The same article at the end listed the team selected for the New Zealand game and low and behold there is no sign of Fennelly. The New Zealand team completed their tour of the country and soon afterwards the Maori touring team arrive to replace them. Up in Brisbane the domestic competition restarts and once more we see no sign of Fennelly in any of the four teams.

We are well into August when the Queensland team to play the Maori tourists in Brisbane is selected and for the first time, we see that Fennelly is down to play on the wing. He played in a trial game on the Saturday 31 July to select the team to play the Maori on the following Saturday. Was he selected based on his reputation as a sprinter of the highest quality who was an experienced rugby union player albeit at a junior level. Whatever the reasons he quickly shows he is up to the job as the reporter wrote ***(Sadly he mis-spelt his name referring to him as S. Fineley).***

"Included in the former team were S. Fineley and A. O'Brien both of whom distinguished themselves."

During the trial Fennelly crossed for the first try and later in the second half crossed once more in a 27-16 win for his team. The question is a simple one, which club was he playing for certainly it was not based in Brisbane. There are a number of possibilities one being there is evidence that up at Mount Morgan there is a club playing the Northern Union code, we know this because Newtown on a tour of the north of Queensland actually played Mount Morgan. However, the Mount Morgan team that faced Newtown did not contain Fennelly. The other problem is that the clubs that the players turned out for are not reported in the newspapers when those players were selected for Queensland.

Whatever the reasons for his selection he did prove the selectors right. On the Saturday the two teams took to the field at the Brisbane Cricket Ground in front of 7,000 supporters in near perfect conditions for rugby league. The first half saw the two packs of forwards strive for dominance but it was Queensland who were in front through tries by Arch Harvey and Nicholson at 8-3. As the first half was coming to a close it was Fennelly who struck. Taking a pass, he sprinted round the outside and outpaced the Maori defence and ran behind the posts to score. With the goal being tagged on the home side went into the dressing sheds leading 13-3.

The second half was barely started when Fennelly repeated the trick. This time taking a pass he simply sprinted down his wing running as straight as an arrow to cross in the corner. In the end the maroons ran out winners by a score of 21-11 much to the delight not only of the home supporters but also the selectors. The two wingmen Fennelly and O'Brien had more than repaid the faith shown in them. The real winner though was the game itself in the northern state, the new code had produced a winning side and this against international opposition. The war with the rugby union was not yet won but a battle had been.

Following the game, the selectors met and selected the team to meet the Maori once more on the Wednesday afternoon. The same thirteen were selected but Duffin moved from centre to five-eight and W. Heidke from five-eight to centre. If the first encounter had begun as an arm wrestle this second encounter was the exact opposite. The ball flew from wing to wing with each side determined to play a fast open game. By half time the home side were leading 17-12 but the Maori were to come back in the second half to take out the game 36-25. While not scoring Fennelly had shown once again just how important speed was in the game of rugby league.

Following the second game Mr Fihelly who had been given full charge of selecting a team to represent Australia against the Maori on the coming Saturday was well aware just what Fennelly was capable of producing on the field. When he announced the team to the press he noted that both Messenger and Courtney had declared they were unable to make the trip up from Sydney to Brisbane for the Test match. However, the three quarter line read, Woodhead, Stuntz, Heidke and Fennelly ***(Even then the newspaper had him down as Feeneley)***

Sadly, when the two teams took to the field at the Cricket Ground for whatever reason Fennelly had been replaced by O'Brien. Research carried out was unable to unearth any reason for that decision but one can only assume it was due to an injury of some description. Or more likely that the reporters got it wrong in the local paper when naming the team. The Test was actually won by the Australians by a score of 16-13. However, it must have been that the selectors were less than happy with the performance and when the Australian team to play down in Sydney the following Saturday was announced Woodhead was on the wing in place of O'Brien. They say one players misfortune is another players opportunity and so that proved to be the case. Woodhead informed the selectors that he could not travel down from Brisbane for the game. The selectors aware of the blistering speed of the Queensland wingman Fennelly selected him to play on the wing as Woodhead's replacement.

Over twelve thousand people were at the Agricultural Showground to witness the encounter and before many of them had actually settled into their seats to enjoy the game Fennelly showed just why he had been brought down from Queensland to play. With the game just a few minutes old Fennelly received a pass while out on his wing and shot away from the cover defenders. When the Maori fullback came to tackle him Fennelly neatly sidestepped him and raced away around the post for the opening try of the game. That score was the first in a game which saw the Australians win by 23-16.

Following the game the reporter writing in the Referee had not missed the importance of Fennelly's effort for he wrote:-

"Fennelly the young Queensland player provided a sensation a minute or so from the kick-off. He fairly flew along the wing and when met by the Maori full back he cleverly sidestepped him and leaving him standing scored behind the posts. He is a player of great promise being handy and unselfish and possessing remarkable speed."

It was a great start to a Test career but many reporters like most supporters on the ground that afternoon were grappling with a bigger mystery, namely who was the faster player, John Stuntz or Sid Fennelly. Both had scored a try through their blistering speed and all wanted to see them run against each other. The reporter in the Referee informed his readers that in the week of the final Test between the two teams it was proposed that both players would run a sprint race in football gear the length of the football field. The race was planned for the Wednesday when NSW and the Maori were to meet but it seems the race never took place.

There was a reason why Fennelly's efforts did not gain the newspaper coverage it deserved or why he himself did not get interviewed. It was that bigger news within the game had broken. The League Secretary Edward Larkin had made the announcement that a good number of rugby union players who had just returned from the tour to England had agreed to switch codes. It was proposed that a series of matches would be played between the Kangaroos and the Wallabies and that was filling the rugby league column inches not Fennelly.

It did seem that Fennelly had impressed the selectors enough for them to retain him in the side for the following Saturday when the Australian and Maori teams were to meet again. On that day things did not go anywhere near as well for Fennelly for while he was fine with the ball in his hand in the first half sadly, he was to sustain an injury. He was injured in the second half and forced to leave the field but the home side still won the game by a score of 20-13. We have no idea just what the injury was or how serious it was. We do know that with the representative season over Fennelly returned from whence he had come namely back into Queensland and obscurity.

It is worth noting at this point that while his rugby league reputation was perhaps growing so too was his reputation as a cricketer. He had a growing reputation as an opening batsman of some quality. So much so he was beginning to attract the attention of the Queensland selectors in that sport also. What we do know is that as the 1910 season up in Brisbane commenced once again there is no sign of Fennelly in any team. It could well be that he was still fulfilling his cricket commitments who knows. To add to the confusion there is a report in The Truth on Sunday 24th July 1910, of a game between North Brisbane and Toombul. The reports states that Fennelly played in that game and scored two tries. However, when the local Brisbane Telegraph in the match report the following day described the game and the teams Fennelly is not in the team. Also, the two tries are actually attributed to Woodhead not Fennelly.

Certainly, he did not figure in the three inter-state games at the end of the season so just where was he, that it seems will remain a mystery. We do know that with the English touring team in Sydney that same year for the first ever Test, Larkin the League Secretary ever the entrepreneur was still trying to arrange a race between Stuntz and Fennelly.

It is the same situation in the 1911 season, no sign of him in the Brisbane competition until once again the inter-state games come around. On Saturday the 29th July a trial match is organized and we see that Fennelly is once more selected to play for the possibles. True to form following the game he is selected to play against NSW the following Saturday. The NSW team came out on top winning 19-9 that afternoon. All the evidence suggests that this representative game was to be his last and he seems to have faded out of the rugby league scene entirely. He did though continue to play cricket at the highest level, representing Queensland twenty one times throughout his career.

However, the newspapers had not finished with Sid Fennelly for we see that while he may well have been a very talented rugby league and cricket player, he was not so successful as a husband. Given that he married in 1909 when he would be just twenty two years old it would not be stretching the imagination too far to believe that his wife was pregnant at the time. We do know that in 1912 he is back in the newspapers when his wife is suing him for not paying maintenance to her and her child. The Truth on the 19th May 1912, carried a humorous account of events in court.

SID. FENNELLY.

(Sketch published in the Truth 19th May 1912)

The evidence suggested by the newspaper was that Fennelly was at the time working as a billiard marker and living in a local hotel. He had been ordered by a Magistrate in October 1911, to pay his wife seven shillings and six pence a week and the same amount for his child but had failed to do so. Interestingly the article referred to Fennelly as a "well known inter-state cricketer." There is no reference to his rugby career. The newspaper actually produced a sketch of Fennelly and attached it to the article. In court he claimed he did not need to pay the money to his wife as she was living with a Mr. Kelly in an adulterous relationship. It was revealed that from the time he married Margaret until the child was born, he paid her only three pounds. Given that his wife was being supported by another man the Magistrate dismissed the summons.

Fennelly continued his cricketing career and we see nothing untoward in his life until 1936 when in August his wife Margaret is in court this time charged with bigamy. It would appear that in 1933 Margaret had married a childhood friend Gilbert Smith. Just three years later following an argument Margaret had phoned the police and confessed to them that she had married Smith but was already married to Fennelly. Gilbert and Margaret were committed for trial on the 5th October 1936.

When the trial was held it was revealed that in 1910 Sid Fennelly had been ordered to pay his wife seven shillings and six pence per week and the same for their child. This he had done so until 1919 when it was agreed that he would pay her a sum of fifty pounds and then no further maintenance would be paid by him. In her defence Margaret Fennelly stated she had not seen her husband from 1923 until January in 1936 when she saw him walking down Queen Street in Brisbane. Prior to marrying Smith, she had made extensive inquiries about her husband's whereabout with no success. After deliberating the jury found her and Smith not guilty and dismissed the case.

Sid Fennelly was in the newspapers once again when his wife sued him for a divorce on the 10th November 1942 some thirty six years after he had married her. That in itself was a comical situation. Margaret was if nothing else unconventional. Having walked from court in 1936 cleared of bigamy just three years later Gilbert Smith had the marriage between them annulled. He used the bigamy trial as a reason and on being successful promptly married another woman. Just a few months later he hired a housekeeper none other than his ex-wife Margaret.

On taking up her duties it did not take her long to discover that Gilbert was actually having an affair with another woman. Margaret informed his wife of the situation and she left filed for divorce and left Gilbert free to marry once again. He decides he wanted to remarry Margaret and so in order to do so she applied for a divorce from Sidney Fennelly hence the court appearance. Margaret revealed in court that on the day she and Sidney had married he took ere back to her parent's house and left to go training for a sprint race telling her he was not prepared to break his contract with

Collingwood. The divorce is granted due to Sidney deserting his wife all those years ago Margaret married Gilbert for the second time and Fennelly simple did what he had been doing, he got on with his own life.

He lived out his life in the Brisbane area until his death on the 25th August 1964. To this day the research carried out by the authors has failed to discover just where Fennelly played his club rugby. He died not knowing or even caring perhaps that he was not considered to be a Kangaroo. After all evidence suggests his first love was cricket. It would be another forty years before The Australian Board of Control would deem the two games he played for Australia against the Maori to be Test matches. That decision changed Fennelly from a No-Hit-Wonder to an Australian Test player. However, when he died, he was not a Test player, so he qualifies for inclusion in the book.

CHAPTER SEVEN

JOE MURRAY
NEWTOWN 1911

It would be true to say that all those who fought in a war were brave men and women. It is also true to observe that some are perhaps braver than others. That was certainly the case for those who served in the Field Company's Engineers during World War One. Members of that and similar companies were possessed of a different not to say special type of courage. The duties of such 'Sappers' was to dig trenches, lay light railway tracks, lines of communication, service trenches and such like. This work was more often than not carried out under the severest of conditions. They tended to be working on or close to the Front Line on the Western Front often under constant enemy fire.

It was one such outfit the 7th Field Company Engineers that Quarter Sergeant Joseph 'Joe' Murray found himself posted to on his enlistment back in 1915. Now just two years on he found himself not for the first time under fire close to the front line of conflict on the Western Front. He and his commanding officer Lieutenant Fewtrell and a squad of Sappers were ordered to layout and excavate a support trench. Fewtrell and Murray went out with rolls of white tape under cover of darkness to layout the trench as they did so they German shell and rifle fire was going on around them.

It was then the job of the sappers with pick and shovel to begin excavating the trench as the firing went on around them. They sought what cover they could and certainly dug down as quickly as they could in order to disappear from German sight. It must have been terrifying as on occasions a German flare would be sent up and as the night sky was illuminated the men would dive for whatever cover they could. There was no way they could really defend themselves as it was difficult to fire a rifle back at the enemy with a shovel in their hands!

It would also have been equally difficult to maintain concentration and fortitude with shells exploding around them with monotonous regularity. It was under these circumstances Murray showed great courage for he constantly moved up and down the line of sappers encouraging them with a quiet word or a pat on the back. He did so at great risk to himself from German fire but in doing so alleviated the fears of his men.

I suppose we should not be surprised at such action as in a time far removed and in more normal activities, he faced similar action playing professional rugby league back in Sydney. When you were on the wrong end of a high score line the opposition had no sympathy, they just kept coming at you. So, it was on the front the German guns did not stop in much the same manner. In both cases all you could do was keep on going.

That was just what Murray did on that long night the shells continued their destructive explosions while the bullets made a much quieter ping as they hit the ground or a stone close by. All night long the sappers dug and Murray cajoled and encouraged and as the first rays of dawn broke the sky line Lieutenant Fewtrell called a halt and he and Murray got their men back to safety. Murray would have felt that he had simply done his job, Fewtrell had a different perspective on his work that night.

On returning to the Company headquarters to write up his report of the nights work he approached his superior officers and explained to them just what Murray had achieved. The result was that Quarter Sergeant Joe

Murray was recommended for the Distinguished Conduct Medal for his gallantry. The recommendation went up the line and on the 2nd July 1917, he was awarded the DCM. The citation read:-

"His Majesty the King has been graciously pleased to approve the award of the Distinguished Conduct Medal to the under mentioned None Commissioned Officer for acts of gallantry and devotion to duty in the field.

No 2776 Quarter Sergeant Joseph Murray

For conspicuous gallantry and devotion to duty. He displayed great coolness and courage in assisting an officer to mark out and excavate a support trench, moving along the line under immense shell fire to encourage the men."

This award was the second oldest in the British Military being introduced way back in 1854 by Queen Victoria as an award for gallantry shown by none-commissioned officers and other ranks. It is second in significant only to the Victoria Cross so was certainly not awarded easily. It also came with a gratuity in this case the sum of £20.

Murray had come a long way from his humble beginnings. He had been born in Cumberland in Sydney in October 1887. He like many boys as they entered their teenage years became interested in the sporting activities of the city. At that time the premier winter activity was rugby union football but by the time he was around twenty years of age the great schism that had ripped the game apart in England arrived in Sydney. He like a great many others watched on with interest at the goings on in the city.

The game of rugby union was rife with rumours half-truths and facts. In 1907 the rumours were that a postal clerk in New Zealand by the name of Albert Baskerville had put together a touring party of high-quality players. He intended to take the party over to the north of England specifically to play the Northern Union clubs, the professional clubs! The half-truths came from the rugby union authorities in Sydney who stated first it was all a huge lie. Then when Baskerville let it be known he was to stop off in Sydney to play a three-match series against Australian opposition the authorities labelled them professionals.

The facts were that James Giltinan, Victor Trumper and Harry Hoyle were the driving force behind a plan to first bring Baskerville to the city. They were also attempting to sign players up to switch codes and join their enterprise. The three also had an ulterior motive namely to start their own league to play the Northern Union brand of football in a league which would be set up for the 1908 season. To that end they were surreptitiously approaching all the top-quality players to join their enterprise and the carrot they dangled in front of them was the opportunity to play against Baskerville's team of New Zealanders.

The twenty-year old Joe Murray was not in that league, not yet and did not warrant an approach from Giltinan. It was early the following year once Giltinan's plan had come to fruition that he became involved. The whole city was buzzing with Northern Union fever. Clubs that had previously played the union code held meetings with a view to setting up a new Northern Union club. One of those meetings was held in Newtown Town Hall on the 8th January 1908 and the instigation of Giltinan. In the eyes of many they were considered to be the first club to switch allegiance. That fact has always been disputed by the Glebe club who claim they were the first to be formed. At the meeting in attendance was the young Joe Murray.

As the inaugural season was approaching the clubs were training hard to get fit and desperately attempting to get to grips with the rules of the new code. To that end Tom McCabe was a great help being probably the only person in the country who had played the professional game. He was charged by Giltinan to hold coaching sessions at all of the newly formed clubs. Murray trained hard but was not to make his first-grade debut until the last round of that first season. At six feet tall and twelve stone eight pounds he was the ideal build for a forward and he could play anywhere in the pack so was to become a useful acquisition for Newtown.

In that initial season Murray was only called upon for first grade duty in the very last round of the season when he took the field against North

Sydney. It was not the most auspicious day as debuts go as he was on the wrong end of a 21-0 score line. The young Murray was playing at prop forward and was obviously up against it all through the game which was played at Birchgrove Oval on the 8th August. The referee that afternoon was the great Tom McMahon. The strange thing was that North Sydney played the match with just eleven men while Newtown played with just twelve men! The paddock was in a terrible state being heavy and greasy which made handling the ball difficult and running even more difficult.

The following season for whatever reasons he was not to play one game for Newtown. The third season was however, as they say a different story. The Newtown club played twelve games during the regular season and he was an ever present. Back prior to 1910 the Premiership was awarded to the team that won through the play-off finals. That changed in that season when the authorities decreed that the two teams that finished first and second on the ladder would play each other with the winner being declared the Premiership winners.

Newtown topped the table with twenty-three points and South Sydney finished in runner up spot with just one point less. So, on the 17th September Murray took to the Sydney Showground in front of fifteen or sixteen thousand supporters in the Grand Final. He was to play prop forward in a powerful front five. Even though the Newtown club had topped the table they were not favourites to take the title. South Sydney had taken out the previous two Premierships and were expected to make it a hat-trick of wins that afternoon.

The game was a low scoring affair with not one try scored in the game. With literally just a few seconds left in the game that Souths were leading 4-2 and Newtown attacking close to the line the Souths centre Howard Hallett collected a loose ball from a scrummage. Given the pressure he was under from the opposition he did well to get his clearing kick away and would have felt that he had won the game for his team. Unfortunately for him the ball sailed straight into the arms of the Newtown centre Albert Hawkes. Having caught the ball cleanly the quick thinking Hawkes as he was entitled to do called for a "fair mark". He was just a few yards inside the Souths half and a few yards in from the touch line. What he had done was give his side a chance, a very slim chance but a chance never the less to kick a goal and draw the match.

The Newtown captain/coach Russell took the ball and in front of a hushed crowd prepared to kick for goal. It was a difficult kick and few on the ground expected him to be successful. Russell as cool as a cucumber stepped up and belted the ball straight through the uprights to tie the game at 4-4. With that the game ended and as his side had ended the season as minor Premiers, they were declared the Premiership winners. They had however been behind all through the game prior to Russell's successful goal. Reading the match reports Murray seems never to have figured prominently in the game. There was nothing new in that for he seemed to be the sort of player every team needs, a tireless worker who would run about all day but his work seemed to always go unnoticed.

The following season took on great significance for Murray and the rest of the players in the league simply because at the season's end an Australian team was to be sent on a second tour to the 'Old Country'. In a determined effort to ensure all had a chance to impress selectors it was decided that a tri-partite competition would be played. New South Wales, Queensland and New Zealand would compete against each other with each game being considered to be a trial match.

There can be little doubt that Murray would not have been filled with confidence at his chances of gaining tour selection. The reason for this was simple he was never selected for the New South Wales team in the competition. He was selected to play for the Metropolis up in Newcastle against Northern Districts on the 22nd June. When the final trial game was played between New South Wales and New Zealand Murray was to play in the preliminary match when the 'A' side were to play the 'B' side. The "A" side being made up of players from clubs occupying odd positions on the ladder while players from the even position formed the "B" side.

With the trial games completed the selectors sat down and selected the players to make the tour. Murray would have been delighted when the squad was announced for he was to join team mates, Neil, V and W Farnsworth, Russell, Noble and McCue on the tour. His Newtown club was providing seven players. There were as to be expected controversies regarding the selections. Added to this was the fact the great Dally Messenger decided to withdraw from the tour and he was replaced by 'Chook' Fraser who was and still is the youngest player to be selected to tour England. There was more upset to follow when the New South Wales Rugby League who were managing the tour refused to endorse the selection of the Queensland forward Nicholson and replaced him by their own selection S. Darmody from South Sydney. It was a crass decision to say the least and a slight to Nicholson and the northern state.

There was worse to follow when it became known in England that Dan Frawley had been selected. The Warrington club over in England claimed he was their player and refused to allow him to play on the tour. The tour managers Ford and Quinlan were determined that Frawley was needed in England and so stated he would go on the tour as a 'trainer'. The plan was to try to alter the Warrington decision once the party were in England. In the midst of all these goings on Murray simply packed his bags ready to set sail for the 'Old Country'.

It must be said that there were many who felt the players had little chance after all the game was only in its fourth year while the Northern Union was in its sixteenth season. As the players sailed north, they did whatever they could on board to maintain fitness as they were determined to be more successful than the previous Giltinan tour. The tour was to open in Coventry and the tourists would be in that city a week prior to the game in order to get their land legs and build up fitness. Joe Murray was no different for while sneaking in by the back door in the eyes of many pundits he was determined to make the most of the opportunity offered to him.

Sadly, he appears to have had little opportunity to do so. The tour began and the tourists took all before them winning the first seven games. Ford and Quinlan the managers seem to have decided that they would play the best thirteen at every opportunity. The result was few changes were made whatever the opposition, I suppose they were mindful of the financial side of the tour. Winning games brought more supporters through the turn stiles to see the Australians toppled. The selection policy was a constant theme that ran through reports back in Sydney in the Referee. The fringe players such as Murray were just that, on the fringes.

The problem posed by the selection of Dan Frawley was one that Ford and Quinlan were desperate to sort out. Warrington were adamant Frawley had signed a three-year contract for which he had received a considerable sum of money. He had played only one year of that contract before returning home where tour manager Quinlan a committee man at his club Eastern Suburbs had allowed him to play even though it was known he was a Warrington player. An underhanded plan was hatched by Ford, Quinlan and Frawley whereby Frawley signed a new contract for the Warrington club and would play for the club at the end of the tour. Sadly, he had no intention of honouring the new contract and having helped his team mates win the Ashes he returned home at the end of the tour.

(The recriminations of this action were to have a profound effect on the Northern Union. The clubs were reluctant to support any further tours to Australia fearing the Australian clubs could and would offer their players a contract and play them as had been the case with Frawley. It took the Northern Union and the NSWRL Secretary Edward Larkin a long time to sort out and the ill feeling generated particularly by John Quinlan led to perhaps the most famous game in the history of the game the Rorke's Drift Test of 1914.)

The tourists were in to their fourteenth game of the tour before he was to get a game and he was not alone for Stuart was in the same boat. Savoury had played only one game on the tour, Darmody just two, Gillett and Burge only three. It was a crazy selection policy but in fairness the squad had defied everyone as they would win the Ashes a feat not performed on English soil again for almost fifty years. Sadly, Murray would pull on a jumper only four times on the tour.

When the tour ended and the players returned home Murray returned to club football with Newtown. In the 1913 season he was selected for the New South Wales tour down to New Zealand. Sadly, international selectors never came calling again and he was destined to fade into the background. When war was declared in 1914, he was still with the Newtown outfit but that was about to change. His father had died and he and his mother moved over to Manly so he was forced to change clubs. The rules as they were at the time stated a player must play for a club in the district that he was residing in.

In the 1915 season he began playing for the North Sydney club turning out in nine games for a very poor side. He was on the winning side just twice. With the season at an end Murray was to walk into a recruitment centre to enlist and do as he saw it his duty. He was two months short of his twenty-eighth birthday and he gave as his next of kin his mother Matilda hence the assumption that his father had died. He joined the 7th Field Company Engineers as his occupation was that of a cooper (barrel maker) the army must have thought he had some engineering experience.

He very quickly rose through the ranks once in the army just a month after enlisting he was promoted to Lance-Corporal. By the time 1917 came around he was Quartermaster Sergeant and leading a squad of men often called upon to perform their work under the most extreme conditions. As we have seen his exploits earned him the second highest honour available in the British military. With the war over and at the age of thirty-three he returned to the game once again with North Sydney.

He played his last game for the club on the 31st July 1920 against University. In that win by thirteen points to three there was a strange irony the game seems to throw up with monotonous regularity. The centre for North Sydney that afternoon was Herman Peters, he also was destined to go on the tour to England but never win a Test place. When Murray ended his playing career he had not finished with the game.

On the 25th June 1921 he was to take to the paddock once more this time with the whistle in his hand. He was to handle the game between ironically Newtown his first club and University. In a career as a referee that spanned over a decade, he would officiate in ninety-seven games. I suppose the highlight of his refereeing career came on the 15th July 1925, when he officiated the game between a University XIII and New Zealand a game the Universities were to win 15-13.

With his refereeing career at an end he did like many before and after him had done he drifted out of the game. To his credit he had been part of history he had been part of that 1911-12 tour that saw the Australians win the Ashes for the very first time and on English soil. Due to the vagaries of a very one eyed not to say myopic selection policy devised by Ford and Quinlan the tour managers he was not to play in a Test. Murray barely played at all in truth while in the Old Country. He was to join the ever-growing number of players who were destined to be No-Hit Wonders of the game. What he did have at the time, was the honour of being one of only two professional rugby league player in the country that had won the Distinguished Conduct Medal.

CHAPTER EIGHT

JOHN KERWICK
SOUTH SYDNEY 1919

John Kerwick must have felt he had really arrived on the rugby league scene in Sydney even if he was making his first-grade debut many a mile from his beloved Redfern and the South Sydney clubs home ground. He had been selected to go on the northern tour of New South Wales and was to take the field against a Murwillumbah River league side up on the Tweed River. The South Sydney club had just clinched the Premiership and had bragging rights over the rest of the league. Kerwick was just two weeks short of his twenty second birthday on that Wednesday 1st July, 1914 that he was to pull on a Souths shirt for the first time as a first grader. During that tour he would make three appearances and score one try.

Sadly, coverage of the tour in the newspapers is a little limited we know that Souths beat Tweed River 35-5, Murwillumbah 33-15, Wallaroos 29-0 and then a Northern Rivers team 28-10 but other matters were occupying newspapers. On the sporting front while Souths were in the northern part of the state England and Australia were playing the 'Rorke's Drift Test down in Sydney and that took precedent. Or more precisely the argument that was raging between the two tour managers and the NSW officials as to whether the third Test would actually be played. On the world stage the assassination of the Archduke Ferdinand in Sarajevo was occupying the front pages. Sadly, the exploits of Kerwick and his South Sydney team mates were not that newsworthy.

His performances must have been enough for the selectors at the club to log him away in their memories for the following season when they would have to defend the Premiership so hard won. Sadly, the world as we had known it had been thrown into chaos thanks to the truculent attitude of the German Kaiser and the British decision to go to war. In that year the horrors of the war had not yet materialised in Australia or in the Old Country for that matter. All thought it was to be a great adventure, something that would be over by Christmas, sadly they were wrong.

As the 1915 season was approaching and a large number of young men had joined the army and shipped out for Egypt the young Kerwick had remained at home and trained hard with his beloved Rabbits. After impressing in the trial games, the selectors felt that he had a number of good qualities not least that of versatility and as the first round of the season came along it was to be tested. The first match was against Glebe and it was to prove an historic occasion for both Kerwick and sadly the world.

On Saturday the 8th May he took to the field to meet a Glebe team. As reigning Premiers, it was expected that South Sydney would easily take the honours. To that end Kerwick was selected to play hooker, the reason for the decision was in all probability due to the fact that Glebe had selected a hooker signed from rugby union who also was making his debut. Sadly, for Kerwick, the Glebe man was a specialist hooker while he was a versatile forward, it cost Souths the match.

With five minutes of the game remaining and the scores locked at 7-7 all expected a tiring Glebe to crumble, they did not. They were to score two converted tries in that last five minutes to take the game. The local reporter did not pull his punches when writing of the game.

"Primarily the success of the wearers of the red jersey was due to the fact of O'Donnell who was making his first appearance as a league player beat the South Sydney hooker almost pointless. The ball came out with monotonous frequency on the Glebe side of the pack."

It was not the most auspicious start to a first-grade career but it was certain the date would live with him and his family from a footballing stand point. It was however a date that would also live in infamy with the rest of the world for it was on that date that a German submarine would sink the Lusitania off the coast of Ireland with catastrophic loss of life! For his part Kerwick must have impressed the selectors as he retained his place in the team not as hooker but rather as a prop. In the following two games he would turn out at lock and then second row. It was this versatility that was his biggest asset at this period in the game. Sadly, as we shall see, later it was to prove his downfall when it came to attempting to win the biggest prize the game has to offer a player.

During that 1915 season the club could not back up on its Premiership win and finished fourth winning eight and losing five with one drawn. However, Kerwick had cemented his place in the side and would go on to become a mainstay of the pack during those war years. He and the club seemed to have mixed fortunes during his time with the club. Premiers in 1914 and then a fourth place finish the following season. The 1916 season saw more drama as that season came to its close.

Throughout the season Balmain and South Sydney had battled to finish top of the table. At the end of the regular season the two clubs could not be separated each winning eleven games. The league ordered the two clubs to play off with the winners to be declared Premiers. The game was played at the Cricket Ground on Wednesday 26th July 1916 and proved to be a close and tight affair. The game turned into the proverbial arm wrestle particularly in the second half when no points were scored. It was not a game of the highest quality with both sides guilty of poor play. Balmain struck first when Halloway scored a try in the corner to take the score to 3-0. In truth they had been the only side in the game in that opening spell. It was then the turn of Souths to launch a series of attacks but they could not break the Balmain defence. The backs had a great deal of ball but slow and at times faulty passing let them down. When Balmain had the ball they were no better and there was a twenty minute spell in the first half when according to the reporter for the Sun **'Play was of the fifth class'.**

Eventually a little football broke out and clever play by Thompson took the ball into the Balmain quarter and Vaughan managed to level the scores crossing for the three points. With the half coming to a close Fraser slotted over a penalty to put Balmain ahead once more 5-3. That was the end of the scoring in the game. The second half saw South Sydney attacking and sadly Oxford missed a couple of easy shots at goal that could have given his side the lead and the Premiership.

Balmain defended brilliantly in the last fifteen minutes of the game, handled everything Souths threw at them to win by 5-3. Kerwick had failed to win a Premiership.

The competition in Sydney at this period was beginning to suffer as a result of the conflict over in Europe but Kerwick and his team mates were still producing good football. During the following season they were once again to finish the season as a bridesmaid rather than a bride as they finished runner up to Balmain yet again. That all changed in 1918 when they took out the Premiership wining twelve games Kerwick actually played in thirteen games for the club so fully earned his Premiership win that season.

As is often the case when a club has a good season, certain players catch the eye of representative selectors. That proved to be the case for Kerwick during the 1919 season. With the war at an end the game was keen to get back into representative football and during that season it was decided that an Australian team would tour New Zealand and play a four match Test series. The Arrow on 8th August listed the players who were to make the tour and amongst them was John Kerwick.

It would be fair to say his selection was not universally accepted as the Cynic wrote in the Arrow:-

"Well I may be wrong but I cannot see where in J. Kerwick has qualified before several others who might be named, men with plenty of ginger and strength in the ruck and go in the open."

Sadly, for the player the very quality that had been his strength at the beginning of his career namely versatility now was a handicap. The game had moved on particularly at the highest level now what was needed was a player who specialised in a single position. A player who was the very best at the job in a single position be it prop, hooker or second row, specialisation was now king. So, it proved to be and Cynic was proved right in his observations.

If Kerwick was a believer in fate then he would have been disquieted even before the tour party left for New Zealand. It must be remembered that the Great War had only just ended and getting berths on a ship for the party was not that easy. The New Zealand authorities wanted the Australian players in the country before the 16th August if possible. The Australian authorities in an effort to accomplish this search up and down the east coast for a ship sailing to Auckland.

They eventually managed to book passage on a steamer leaving Newcastle on Tuesday the 12th August. They transported the players up to Newcastle and got them aboard the ship. It was then things went wrong because one of the boilers on the steamer burst! The players had to remain in Newcastle until another steamer could be found. They eventually sailed from Newcastle for Auckland on Friday 15th August it was not a good omen for the players in general and Kerwick in particular.

On that tour across the Tasman Sea Kerwick would pull on the green and gold jersey three times but never in any one of the four Test matches played. The players actually arrived by steamer into Wellington on Friday 22nd and a number of the players were suffering from leg injuries they had carried over from the domestic competition. The following day they were to play the first game of the tour. It was a strange tour in so much as the first four games of the tour were in actual fact Test matches between the two countries.

The Australians prevailed 44-21 in the first encounter which was a fantastic achievement as they had only arrived the day before after being at sea for six days. In total the tourists scored ten tries in a great display and in truth the home side never looked like winning the game. Following such a display as was to be expected changes would not be made. Consequently, Kerwick along with other players could do little else but train and hope.

That game completed the tour move down to Christchurch and prepared for the second encounter between the two countries. In the second Test however, it was the home side that came out on top 23-10 in a wretched game. The pitch was heavy and the referee did not endear himself to the visitors with his display and some of his decisions were labelled as ludicrous by the Australians. There was no doubt that on the day the better side won and the New Zealand forwards out played their opposition. That being the case Kerwick and others would have held out hopes of a Test call up as changes could and should have been made. Sadly, that was not to be, changes were made in the forwards but Kerwick did not figure. Bill Schultz came into the side at prop for the third encounter following the loss and retained his place in the final Test.

The third Test was played in Auckland and a record crowd of 21,000 turned out to witness the encounter. The Domain Ground was in perfect condition for rugby league a far cry from the pitch in Christchurch and the Australians used it to perfection winning the game 34-23. The game did have its moments and just ten minutes into the second half the Australian second row Watkins was ordered from the field. According to reports his open hand made contact with the face of an opposition forward and the referee deemed it serious enough to send him off. Mind you he did level up the numbers a little later when he ordered the New Zealand forward Waters off for rough play.

The tourists won the third match with ease and with it the rubber, surely now was the time to see what the fringe players could do at this level. The selectors did make one change in the pack with Oxford coming in for Ryan but there was no place for Kerwick. For Kerwick it was a case of so near yet so far. He had made it into the tour party but not the Test run on side. He actually made his debut for his country on Thursday 23rd September 1919 against Waikato a game the Australians won 58-5 and Kerwick would cross for a try. Just four days later he would take to the field once again against Hawkes Bay and he would score another try in a 67-4 victory. His final appearance in the green and gold jumper came in a 93-5 win over Wellington a game in which he played second row.

The question must be asked why was Kerwick taken over to the Dominion when he was never really given an opportunity to show just what he was capable of at the highest level. After all he was only twenty-seven years old and at the top of his game. He had been selected to play in three none Test matches against opposition that was so weak it would be difficult to judge if Kerwick had the ability to succeed at international level.

The selectors preferred Bill Schultz the Balmain prop when changes had to be made in the front row for the Test matches. With the series almost won surely the selectors would be looking to the future and seeing if the younger players had the ability to perform at the highest level. Kerwick never got that opportunity. Sadly, he was not the first player to suffer from the vagaries of selectors and he would not be the last. It is hard to understand the thinking of selectors at international level but it was as true then as it is today. It is hard to get into the international side but much harder to get dropped from the team!

On his return home international duty eluded him as he seems to have never figured in the selector's minds for whatever reasons and he settled back into club football. Schultz on the other hand went on to play Test rugby against England on their tour in 1920 and then toured England on the 1921-22 visit. Such are the vagaries of Test selectors had Kerwick got the nod then he not Schultz could well have gone on to international success sadly it was not to be. Kerwick played on until the end of the 1922 season and at the age of thirty for whatever reasons his career came to an end, he had played eighty-three games for South Sydney and three for Australia albeit none of them Test matches. So, he like many others who would follow him was destined to be yet another 'No Hit Wonder.'

CHAPTER NINE

HERMAN PETERS NORTH SYDNEY 1921

The beauty of rugby league clubs and their supporters is that once in a while the Gods smile upon them with regard to the number of great players that come to a club at the same time. When that happens, great things tend to follow both for the club, the players and also its supporters. For the "Shoremen" that are the North Sydney club the Gods really smiled on them at the beginning of the 1920s. It was then that the club had a three-quarter line second to none in the game at that time. The names run off the tongue with ease, Horder, Rule, Peters and Blinkhorn and they terrorised the opposition. Of this quartet a reporter later was to write:-

"Few line-ups in premiership history are as fabled as the 1921-22 North Sydney side. The long-suffering club's only Premiership winning outfit."

Sadly, one of the famous four was destined to become yet another 'No Hit Wonder' of the game and a controversial figure.

Herman Peters was born on the North Shore in Sydney in 1899 so it was only natural that he would gravitate to the North Sydney club once he began playing the game. He very quickly gained a reputation as a player with great attacking skills and with an eye for even the smallest opening. Such was his talents that when just eighteen in 1917 he ran out at Birchgrove Oval on Saturday 25th June, to make his first-grade debut. His centre partner that afternoon was Ces Blinkhorn. Sadly, it was not the dream debut he would have hoped for as it turned out Balmain ran away with the game winning 25-2. Peters would make just four appearances for the club in that 1917 season.

What quickly became apparent was that while his attack could not be faulted defensively, he was it must be said just a little frail. Sadly, it was a perceived frailty that would remain with him throughout his entire career and perhaps rob him of the highest honour in the game. However, the following season he would make twelve appearances either at full back or on the wing as he set about learning his craft in this tough environment that was Sydney rugby league. It was not a happy season for him as he was on the winning side just three times. If that were not bad enough the following season 1919 saw him make thirteen appearances and win just once as the club took the wooden spoon. Things got a little better the following year when he was on the winning side six times during the campaign.

It was then that the Gods smiled on the club for in 1921 the coach the great Chris McKivat was able to put on the field Horder, Rule, Peters and Blinkhorn who were guided around the paddock by the scrum half Duncan Thompson. We had seen glimpses of the potential the previous season in games but there was a lack of consistency, McKivat put that fault right. During this shortened campaign the club and Peters were to go undefeated with seven victories and one draw. The reason for the short season was that the Australians were to tour the Old Country and would need to leave toward the end of June.

As is ever the case when a club is having great success it is they who seem to have greater representation in state or national sides. North Sydney were no different when the tour party trials were announced at the end of the 1921 season. A number of trial games were arranged involving NSW teams the first was against New Zealand on a Saturday. For that game Blinkhorn and Rule were selected to play. The second game which was played on the following Monday was against Queensland and in that encounter Horder was selected to play while Peters was to be a reserve.

It would be the end of June when the team to tour England was finally announced and for the first time there was not one New Zealand player in the squad. This could truly be termed an Australian team. From the North Sydney club view point it fully justified their season as six of the Premiership winning side had gained selection. Sadly, for whatever reason the centre Rule did just that, he ruled himself out of making the long trip back to the Old Country. Peters was just twenty-two years old and had managed to force himself into the tour squad. Claude Corbett writing in the Sun said of the selection:-

"The inclusion of Peters (N.S.) and Brown (Q) and even Carstairs (St. G.) proves that the selectors have not been blind to promise and merit."

Peters had the rugby world at his feet and he would have had high hopes that a green and gold Test jersey was his for the asking. True while his attacking prowess was not in dispute there was still that nagging question with regard to his defence. The North Sydney coach Chris McKivat had used the attacking strength of his three quarters to such effect that defence took second place. At international level however, defence was just as important as attack if not more so particularly against the old enemy.

When the tour party arrived in England and began playing their games Peters had to wait his turn for selection. It seems that the selectors had once again adopted a policy of defining a first and second squad. The young Peters was looked upon as second string and so was forced to sit out game after game on the tour. It was the 2nd November before he took to the field against York for his first outing. It was a game best forgotten as the home side took the spoils 9-3. The game was eventful with one Australian, the hooker and a couple of York forwards getting an early bath. Peters for his part with the game coming to a close managed to get the ball with a little space to work in. He stepped inside his marker and sped out to the wing and raced to the try line. Sadly, his moment of glory was halted by a cover tackle that took him, the defender and the corner flag out into touch.

He was a little luckier when he took the field against Barrow a few weeks later this time playing on the wing. When he did get the opportunity on the field once again, he quickly showed why he had been brought to the Old Country scoring a blistering try from the half way line with no one getting near to him. Sadly, the Gods were still not smiling on him as he was to suffer an injury to his shoulder and was to play only four games on the tour scoring three tries. The elusive Test cap had eluded him.

He was however on the scene to witness perhaps one of the most despicable acts the game had endured to that time. The Australian manager S. G. Ball wanted to play an exhibition game in France and to that end travelled over to Paris. There he arranged for a game to be played at the Pershing Stadium. It was then that the French Rugby Union Authorities stepped in. They exerted pressure on the sporting authorities and were successful in ensuring that the tourists would not be allowed access to a stadium in Paris suitable to stage the match.

Harry Sutherland writing in the Sun on the 28th January 1922 summed up the whole shameful episode:-

"The possibilities of a boycott by the Sporting Federation of France, organised by the Rugby Union in the first instance, has made it difficult for the Northern Union to secure a suitable ground for the

match. Mr S. G. Ball one of the Australian managers crossed over to Paris armed with a letter from the English Soccer Authorities in the hope of securing a soccer ground but even in these quarters the authorities professional and all as they are, have an agreement with the bodies that embrace the amateurs and Mr Ball returned from Paris with such a report that the match was abandoned."

It appeared that Peters and a number of other players travelled with Ball to France on that occasion. It was a most shameful act by the rugby union authorities and must have been particularly galling to those players who had seen action in the recent war. The French and Australians has fought side by side in the war against the Germans now they could not take to a rugby field to play a game in the country they had supported for three or more years. What is even more surprising is that Peters in his diary of the tour suggests that when Ball returned from Paris to England, he had information that the English rugby union authorities were colluding with their French counterparts to ensure the game was not allowed to go ahead. If true it is a damning indictment on the English rugby union given what had transpired from 1914 to 1918 when English and Australians had fought side by side against the might of Germany.

Given events in Paris at that time we should not then be surprised by the action of the very same French authorities during the Second World War. When the Germans invaded France and the Vichy Government was set up, the rugby union officials approached the authorities in the Vichy Government organisation. They successfully persuaded them to abolish the rugby league game in the country. Not only that but they took over all the assets of the rival code. Even to this day they have steadfastly refused to compensate the league game for that monstrous illegal injustice. Also, if Peters assumptions are correct it shows just how deep were the feelings of the rugby union authorities to the new code even though by then it was some twenty-five years old.

On his return to Sydney in 1922 Peters and the club continued where they had left off in the league. Once again, they were in the forefront and Peters would play seventeen games. In the last game of the season which was won to clinch a second Premiership the famed three quarters really went to town. They absolutely demolished Glebe winning 35 to 3. What made the game stand out above all the other games that season was that the North Sydney three-quarter line scored all of those 35 points with Rule, Blinkhorn and Horder crossing for two tries each. Peters chipped in with one and Horder slotted over seven goals.

Unfortunately, the representative selectors were still not convinced about Peters defensive qualities and the game had moved on since his debut and more and more defence was looked on as the key to success. It would be 1923 before he was to gain selection for New South Wales in the match against Queensland. Ironically it was Monday the 25th June when he ran out onto the Sydney Cricket Ground six years to the day since he had made his club debut. Sadly, the result was the same as Queensland triumph by 18-13. The selectors still had problems with his defence and had selected him to play on the wing rather than his favoured position in the centre.

It appeared that almost to a man, reporters of the game considered Peters to be the best centre in New South Wales. Sadly, the selectors thought differently back in 1924 when he failed to gain selection for the state side, there was an outcry. His position was exacerbated even further when his club selected him to play on the wing. He refused to turn out feeling to do so would affect his chances of representative honours against the English who were to tour that season. Claude Corbett wrote in the Arrow of the club and Peters:-

"Peters is a great centre and a man whom we need against the Englishmen and Queensland if Horder and Blinkhorn are to get chances to score."

Peters would never again pull on a representative jersey and in 1925 when once more he was passed over by the state selectors Corbett again had his say this time in the Sun:-

"There is no doubt in my mind that the reason the selectors have passed over Peters is that they do not think his defensive powers are good enough for today's New South Wales teams."

As the season came to its end it proved to be his last in the game as a player. At a meeting of the club in March 1926 he announced his retirement from the game. Many thought this was due to his constantly being passed over by representative selectors but he himself stated that he had "a doubtful leg". When the famous three quarter-line had been broken up success left the club and Peters who had captained the side called it a day. He would return to the club as coach in 1934 but was unable to secure a Premiership for the club once more. Peters would go on to become a selector for the Australian Rugby League in 1948 and was once again involved in one of the biggest controversies in the game's history this time as a selector.

He was one of the selectors for the Kangaroos 1948-49 tour to England and was involved in the sacking or should that more accurately be the none selection of the incumbent international coach and skipper Len Smith, replacing him by Col Maxwell. Given Smith had led the Australians to victory in a Test against New Zealand just a week prior to the tour side being announced all thought he was a shoo in for selection. After all he had been selected as captain coach by the same selectors that were to select the twenty-eight players who would travel to England.

Sadly, he was not selected and rumours abounded. It was felt in some quarters that Smith a Catholic had not been selected as the majority of the selectors were Protestants and Freemasons to boot. At that time both here and back in England the Freemasons was very much a Protestant organisation due in part to antagonism from the Catholic Church who looked upon masonry as a 'secret' organisation. Once over in England Smith would as captain have had to deal with English club directors a good many of whom were not Catholic and just as importantly members of a Freemasons Lodge. Perhaps the feeling was that he would not sit well in the company of club directors. It is and was incomprehensible that the sitting skipper and coach of the national team just a week previously should not even be selected in the two sides for a tour to England.

If Peters thought the decision to drop Smith would cause little or no furore, he was sadly mistaken. Just a few days after the tour team was announced he was forced to justify the decision as an article in the Sun on 25th June showed.

"Chairman of the Australian Rugby League (Mr Herman Peters) said today there was no victimisation in the omission of Test captain Len Smith from the team to tour England.

"Selection of the team was above board" said Mr Peters. He added. "The selectors have not yet prepared a statement. However, we are prepared to do so if the Board of Control wants us to answer Newtown Secretary Dave Jolley's accusations of victimisation. We are standing by our selection. Unless the Board of Control calls for an inquiry the whole incident is closed and we have nothing further to say."

There is no doubt that there were some shenanigans going on when the incumbent Test skipper who had led the team to victory just a week or so earlier not only lost the captains role but also a place in the tour team. Given Peters past history being on the receiving end of selectors whims he must have been only too aware of just how his decision would affect Len Smith. Two teams were effectively selected for that tour and Smith was not considered good enough to gain a place in either of them. It was and still is a stain on the Australian game even after all these years.

It would be many years before another side to this whole sorry saga was to emerge and it suggested that there were even more sinister reasons behind Smith not making the tour. In 1995 Wally O'Connell wrote in his autobiography 'In Defence" that it was not religion but rather politic and a great mistake on the part of the selectors. As O'Connell wrote Norm Robinson who was at the time the NSW coach wanted the coaching job for the 1948 tour. He was to play a part in the intrigue the other problem came from a selection gaffe or should that be a lack of truth.

The selectors for what ever reason had selected three centres for the tour and Len Smith was not amongst them. The selectors could not agree on the fourth centre some wanting Smith others wanting the Queenslander Horrigan. In such cases when the voting was tied the matter was referred to an arbiter. That arbiter was Jerry Brien and it was a well known fact that he felt Horrigan was the best centre in Australia at the time. He was brought into the room and asked to give his vote Smith or Horrigan. O'Connell felt that in making that decision Brien did not know he was voting for the last centre spot on the tour. It was his vote that decided Smith's fate. Robinson did not get the coaching role Cal Maxwell was appointed captain coach for the tour. O'Connell felt that Smith was the victim of another man's greed and ambition.

Whatever the reasons for the controversy it was a decision that was to stay with Peters for the rest of his time in the game. It is a stain on the game that remains to this day.

Peters died on the 10th September 1989 at the age of ninety. He had gained every honour the game had to offer up to that time, bar one. While he went on tour in 1921 that elusive Test jumper eluded him. He was destined to be one more 'No Hit Wonders' of the game.

CHAPTER TEN

EDDIE ROOT SOUTH SYDNEY 1929

On the afternoon of the 30th November 1929, in Swinton in the north of England it was cold, wet and foggy. At the Station Road ground Australia were playing the home team Swinton. The first half had proved a great test for the visiting team but they had slowly gained the upper hand in spite of the conditions. They had scored the only try of the game in that first half and led by 5-2. In the second half that lead had been cut to a single point and as was inevitable in such circumstances, tempers became frayed.

The battle in the forwards had been just that a battle, in the main mostly within the rules of the game. Slowly that changed and fist fights broke out which tried the patience of the referee. It was after one such scuffle that Eddie

Root heard the shrilled sound of the referee's long blast of his whistle. Root had been in a scuffle with an opposing forward and had got a good one in that had rocked his opponent back. As the players were separated by team mates the referee stood away from the scuffle and pointed a finger at Root.

He knew full well the outcome was not going to be good and so it proved to be. The referee had been tried just once too often and after a short lecture he pointed Root in the direction of the dressing room and ordered him off for an early bath. As he was leaving the field Root looked back to see Hodgson the Swinton forward placing the ball to kick at goal from the penalty he had conceded. Sure enough the ball sailed through the uprights and all the Australian hard work had been undone as the home side took the lead 6-5. It was a lead they would never lose and as the game was coming to a close Swinton crossed for a try to seal the victory 9-5.

It was not the first time Root had received his marching orders in a big game. Three years earlier in the Grand Final South Sydney had topped the table and made it through to the finals. There they had disposed of the Eastern Suburb side quite easily by a score of 21-5. In the final they were to meet University and all expected them to have an equally easy win but that proved not to be the case. In the final with the score standing at 11-0 to South Sydney the Rabbitohs launched an attack which was only halted a few yards from the University line.

As the players began scrummaging for the ball there was a bit of a scuffle involving a number of players from each side. One of them was Root and he was pulled out by the referee Webby Neill who was a former Premiership winner with South Sydney. Inexplicably he gave Root his marching orders and very few on the field or the ground felt the punishment fitted the crime. Luckily Souths a man short held on to take the Premiership winning 11-5 that day.

On that cold foggy afternoon in Swinton Root had time to contemplate just what he was doing in the north of the 'Old Country' and how he had come to be there. It was a far cry from those early days when as a youngster he had simply played the game of rugby league for the fun of it. Given his upbringing it was hardly surprising that he was known in the game for not taking a backward step. On the paddock Eddie Root was happy to play the game whichever way the opposition wanted it, open play or skulduggery.

Way back in 1902 in the Waterloo suburb of Sydney on 5th October Edward Root first saw the light of day. Given the next suburb along was Redfern, when he was growing up and the South Sydney club had come into existence when he was just six years old that became his club. Having supported them little did he know that he would eventually join the playing ranks of the club. Before then a lot was to happen in his young life that would shape his personality both on and off the field.

As he grew to young adulthood he developed into a powerful unit and while playing his junior football was always placed in the pack. He was both strong and quick and also became a more than competent goal kicker. Any thoughts of playing the game professionally were far from his mind when on the 1st March 1915, his mother sadly passed away. The thirteen-year old boy was then left in the care of his father James and together they went on with the everyday job of living.

Worse had preceded this when in 1914, the world was thrown into chaos following the outbreak of the first World War. Eddie like many throughout the world looked on that event as the opportunity to take part in a 'great adventure'. As the war progressed and reality kicked in it seemed the horrors were to have little or no effect on Root who felt he should be doing his bit. Much as he would have liked to join in the war effort, he was sadly too young. He was however not going to let a small thing like age hold him back.

Either with or without his father's blessing on the last day in March 1917 he marched into the recruitment office in Newtown and enlisted. According to his service record he was eighteen years and two months old, five foot six inches in height and weighed just shy of ten stone. He told the recruiting officer that he had been born in Alexandria in the county of Cumberland in Sydney. He also stated that he had served as a senior cadet for four years. On the application form there is the signature of his father James so we can assume either the person who accompanied him was not his father. On the other hand, it could well have been that his father was complicit in his son's determination to enlist. Given all the information and his excellent physical health he was admitted into the army as private, service number N76203. The problem was that at that time he was just fourteen years and five months old and yet he had convinced experienced recruitment officers that he was eligible to serve in the army.

Sadly, try as he may he could not keep up the pretence when he was in the service, checks were made and he was discharged as being under age just seventeen days later. You can but admire the courage of one so young who was determined to do his duty not only for King and Country but for Australia. Having been discharged he went back to the mundane every day working life at that time. He told the recruiting officer that his occupation was that of a clerk but that was probably also untrue.

Just a year later thankfully the war came to an end and Root had settled back into life in Sydney, working and playing rugby league. Thankfully he filled out as all youngsters do and became a forward in the game with a reputation for taking no nonsense. He was also a player of some skill and ability and in the early 1920s he came to the attention of the South Sydney club officials who saw his as a player of potential. They were not wrong in their assessment and in 1923 at the tender age of twenty-one he made his first-grade debut for his beloved South Sydney club.

The opposition that Saturday afternoon the 11th August at the Sydney Cricket Ground Number 2 were the Newtown 'Bluebags'. There were around 1,500 watching as ironically Webby Neill the referee blew to start the game. The game must have been a dream come true for young Root as Newtown were defeated 25-7 and not only that he crossed for a try on debut, it did not get any better than that. Sadly, coverage of the game is sparse to say the least so we have little or no idea of how well Root played or how he scored his try.

Root helped the club to share first place on the ladder come the end of the season they and Eastern Suburbs tied. The League ordered a final play off final and Easts won the game 15-12 to take out the Premiership. Root who was just breaking into the first grade was not selected for that game. The following season the same thing occurred only this time Balmain finished tied with Souths on fifteen points each. On this occasion Root did play in the final only to see his team lose out by the narrow score of 3-0. It was however becoming a golden era for the club and for him.

The following year 1925 Souths took all before them and ended the season with an undefeated record, played twelve, won twelve and Root had his first Premiership under his belt. They would retain the Premiership in 1926 in spite of having Root dismissed in the final against University. The success was continued into the next season when Root and the Rabbits topped the ladder yet again winning fourteen games. In the play-off finals they met Western Suburbs and disposed of them with ease going into the final by a score of 38-6. In the final they played St George and came away with yet another title winning 20-11. Root actually crossed for a three pointer in the game.

The following season it appeared that the bubble had burst for South Sydney in the league as they could only manage third spot on the ladder. When the final series came around it saw the same old Souths. They met ladder toppers St George in a repeat of last season's final but this time in the semi and came away with a 13-5 win to take them into the final yet again. This time the opponents were runners up Eastern Suburbs and Souths simply blew them away taking the title 26-5. All seemed to be rosy in Root's garden in terms of his football career.

In 1929 the South Sydney club took out its fifth consecutive Grand Final beating Wests in the semi-final with ease and Newtown in the final with an even easer win. All of this was achieved without Eddie Root as he was elsewhere going on to bigger and better things as they say. He was on the Orsova bound for England along with the rest of the players selected to represent Australia on the 1929-30 tour. How he got on the tour was another story as they say.

It started with him gaining selection for the New South Wales State team which he did in June 1927. He was twenty-five years old and probably in that purple patch all top players seem to experience. His club South Sydney were riding high and along with them was Root and a number of other club mates. Given the circumstances it is only natural that the selectors would look closely at such players and Root got the nod.

On the 25th June he strode onto the Sydney Cricket ground in the sky-blue jumper in front of 56,000 supporters to face a strong Queensland outfit. In truth the selectors had to some extent been forced into changes after the drubbing they had received at the hands of the maroons in the encounters last season. The game turned out well and truly to be an arm wrestle and Root was amply suited for such a game. The Queensland pack to a man were bigger than their opposite numbers but when the game began the sky-blue forwards tackled like demons constantly knocking back their opponents.

It seemed inevitable that the bigger and more experienced Queensland outfit would take control of the game. They took control of the scoring but not the opposition and at half time the home side were behind by 10-4 having given up two tries. The ray of hope for the sky-blue outfit was they would have the benefit of the strong wind in the second half. It was a piece of work by Root that really got his team back into the wrestle. As the reporter for the Referee 'The Cynic' wrote:-

"The ball was in the ruck at the 25. It went forward some yards, and Root fielding it was pronounced off side by most people. It looked off side, but, as I could not see whence the ball shot off low from the rucking players, I could not say definitely that it was. Root passed out to his mate on the right wing, and he gave it to Wearing, who dodged Caples, beat two others who tried to grab him, and then fell across the line to score in the corner."

That vital first score took the score closer at 10-7 and it was then all to play for and Root and his pack mates were up for it. A penalty closed the score still further to 10-9 and when a field goal sailed over for the first time NSW had the lead at 11-10. A few moments later Root was crucially involved once again as the reporter noted:-

"From the drop out and Blair fielding the ball outside his 25, started on one of the South Sydney movements forward. Wearing on the wing joined with his forwards, and finally Root took the pass clear of opposition, to run in and score on the right wing."

The conversion was missed but the lead had stretched out to 14-10 and just a couple of minutes later the referee blew to end the game. As debuts go Root's was pretty good and he was to cement a place in the state side for a good many years on the back of that initial outing. He was becoming a forward who was both versatile and more importantly consistent in his performances.

Mind you it was not all plain sailing for Root as the following season proved. The highlight of the 1928 season was to be the tour by the Englishmen and the first serious game of that tour was to be played out in Sydney when NSW played the tourists. When the team was announced for the game Root was not in the side. The state side beat the Englishmen 20-15 in that game and so were not expected to make any changes for the next encounter.

The selectors had other ideas and just two days later on the King's Birthday when the two teams met once more Root was called into the team as one of three replacements in the pack and two in the backs as the selectors looked at other players. Sadly, the English turned in a much better performance this time and won going away by 24-9. When the team was announced for the third encounter on the Saturday the selectors named seven forwards with one to be omitted from the team. Root was not one of the seven named. Just a couple of weeks later when the Australian team to play the first Test was named Root was again absent.

The following season was an equally important one internationally as the Australians were to send a tour party over to the north of England. That meant the interstate games took on greater importance as they would be viewed as tour trial games. In the first two games again played on a Saturday and a Monday NSW triumphed and Root played well so must have held out hope that he had done enough to gain tour selection. When NSW won the third encounter pundits speculated as to which players would be in the party, few if any named Root but his team mate Treweeke was on everyone's lips.

Root having been involved in the NSW interstate games must have felt that on the evening of the 29th June when the selectors met that he had a chance. So, it turned out to be for when the twenty-six names were announced to his delight, he was one of them. He was one of five players from the South Sydney club the others being Harry Finch, Harry Kadwell, Paddy Maher and George Treweeke. He was on his way to the Old Dart and the possibility of an Australian cap was in his own hands.

On gaining selection and in the resulting publicity Harry Sunderland writing in the Brisbane Courier gave thumb nail sketches of the tourists. His opening comments on Root are quite illuminating:-

"Edward Alexander Root of South Sydney says he is twenty seven years of age and yet he wears a returned soldiers medal. He must have enlisted when he was very young for the war has been over eleven years now."

As we know he was only fourteen when he enlisted and served only three weeks or so in the forces before being retuned home.

The players actually sailed across the Pacific stopping at Honolulu before sailing on to Vancouver in British Columbia. After a day of sightseeing the players then boarded a train bound for eastern seaboard of Canada and then a ship to England. On that tour Root was to play fifteen games but sadly he was never to figure in a Test match. He actually played in two of the first five tour matches all of which were won quite easily as was to be expected. He was to play his second game against Widnes and would have been pleased with his performance. The selectors were at least giving players as much football as they could to get them all in good condition. There were two worries though one was the low attendance at games which affected the coffers and the other was the opinion formed by the English press that the forwards were not of the standard expected of an Australian side.

From a personal point of view the big worry for Root was that on the first big outing of the tour the game against Lancashire he was not in the team.

It was a game the Australians won 29-14 and even at this early stage the writing seemed to be of the wall for Root. In the next game at Wakefield a weaker side containing Root went down to the home side 14-9 it was the first defeat suffered by the tourists. With the first Test match at Hull upon them Root was not to figure in the front row. In that game the Australians turned on a magnificent display and ran England ragged winning the game 31-8. Root would have felt that in order to get into that Test team he would have to rely on players getting injured.

This tour had one unique feature and was simply the need for the first time ever for a fourth Test match. Having won the first Test the tourists they went down in the second by a score of 9-3 which set up a nail biting third encounter as the winner would take the Ashes. That third game was played at Station Road Swinton and resulted in a 0-0 draw. It was a game steeped in controversy and there is little doubt the tourists were robbed of a victory. With little time remaining from a scrum the Australian scrum half 'Chimpy' Busch picked up from the scrum and went on his own on the blind side running for the corner. He flew over the try line for what he and everyone on the ground thought was the Ashes winning try. In the very act of scoring the English loose forward covering across Fred Butters tackled Busch and as he did so the corner flag was knocked over.

At this time, it needs to be pointed out that unlike today the corner flag was in play so if you hit it, it was deemed that you were in touch. While the referee thought a try had been scored and told the Australian player such, he could not over rule his touch judge who had raised his flag and stated the player was in touch before he had been able to get the ball down. The controversy over that none score rages on even today. It was the first and only time a Test between the two countries has ended scoreless. As it stood the English had retained the Ashes having drawn the series it was though a hollow victory in the eyes of the authorities.

To settle the matter a fourth Test was hastily arranged at Rochdale and played on 15th January. That game saw the English win 3-0 and with it take the Ashes. So, it was four Test matches were played for the first time ever and Root was not to figure in any of them. That seemed to be the case for the rest of the tour, in the club matches Root was to figure but in the big occasions he was keeping a seat in the stand warm. While he was over in England the authorities back home were conspiring to provide Root with yet another upset.

At the end of the 1929 season the New South Wales authorities rearranged the district boundary lines associated with each club. Back then a player had to play for the club in whose district they resided. Root was South Sydney through and through but when the new boundaries were announced he found his home had been placed into the district associated with the Newtown club. Both he and his wife who was also a big Rabbitohs supporter were devastated at the news but could do little about the situation.

On his return from the tour as he prepared for the following season, he and his wife made plans to get him back to the South Sydney club. They promptly put their feelers out to move into a house in the Souths district which they did and the following season he moved back into a green and red jersey. He would remain at the club until the end of the 1933 season. He was never selected for the national squad again even though he continued to play for the NSW state side until the end of the 1932 campaign.

After a couple of years out of the game he was persuaded to join the St George club which he did and acted as captain coach for the red vee. At the end of the 1936 season he was under such pressure from his occupation that he decided to retire from the game which he did. Root was a fiercely competitive character who had such a nationalistic streak that even as a fourteen year old boy, he had managed to persuade experienced army recruitment officers back in 1917 that he was actually eighteen and fit to serve his King and country in the fight against the German army might.

He had served his country on the 1929 tour playing fifteen times for the green and gold but he never received the very highest honour that of representing Australia in a Test match. It is for this reason that Root was to join the ranks of those players who we are classifying as 'No Hit Wonders'.

Eddie Root died on the 15th May 1986 at Brighton-le-Sands he was eighty-four years old.

CHAPTER ELEVEN

RAY MORRIS
UNIVERSITY 1933

The career of Ray Morris is perhaps the saddest story in the history of the game of rugby league be it in Australia or any other country where the game is played. He was born in Ashfield in Sydney ironically on the 4th April in 1908 the year the game's first official league programme began. Throughout his career there were similar ironies with his playing career.

As he grew from boyhood to manhood so did his stature. By the time he attracted the attention of the selectors for the Western Suburbs club he was close to six feet tall and weighed in at thirteen stone eight pounds. He began his career playing for the third-grade side. His strong straight running and fierce hand off quickly made him a handful for the opposition. It was not long before he was knocking on the door of the first-grade squad.

He made his debut in the first grade in round 15 on the 13th August 1927, he was just nineteen years of age. I suppose the old maxim 'if you are good enough you are old enough'. Was adopted by the club. The opponents that day were the University Club. There was a certain irony about that which will be revealed later. It was a game that saw him on the winning side as Wests overcame University 21-13. In that season he would pull on a first-grade jumper five times and in his last scored a try his first points for his club.

The following season he would make eight appearances playing on the wing or full back as well as in the centre. He was however growing a reputation as a player who was going to be one of the new stars of the game, a player who could well help wrest the Ashes from the Englishmen. It was to be in his fourth season with the club he really came of age as it were.

The 1930 season saw the club finish on top of the ladder finishing two points ahead of Easts and six ahead of the reigning Premiers South Sydney. In the finals they defeated Souths winning 9-5. In the minor final they actually lost to St George going down 14-6. However due to the system in place at that period as minor premiers they got a second bite of the cherry and when the two teams met on the 4th October at the Sydney Sports Ground it was Wests who took the honours winning 27-2.

Morris played on the wing that afternoon and according to reports was a constant thorn in the side of St. George he scored one try and made a couple more for his team mates and at the age of just twenty-two he had won a premiership. The following season saw him make his debut for New South Wales on the 6th June 1931. It was a game that cemented Morris as a player with both attacking and defensive qualities at the highest level. That afternoon he crossed for two tries playing on the wing in a 39-17 defeat of Queensland.

The following season which was to be his last with the club saw success come his way once more. On the ladder they finished runners up to

South Sydney winning eleven games. In the finals they faced Balmain and disposed of them 15-7 and so went on to meet South Sydney whom they defeated easily 23-8. However, the system in place at that time the so called 'right of challenge' ensured that Souths got the right to have a second bite of the cherry. This time the result was reversed when after a titanic struggle Souths took out the Premiership winning 19-12.

The game was played on the 24th September at the Sydney Sports ground and with the half time score 9-2 in favour of Souths the game seemed over. In the second half Wests battled back to level the score at 12-12. It took a massive penalty by Benny Wearing to give the lead back to Souths and when late on Lewis crossed for a converted score the game was lost. It proved to be the last game Morris would play for the club. He was in the wars during the final for when going for the line in a heavy tackle he was cut over his left eye and needed treatment on the touchline. Try as he may he could not get his team across the line. The ironic thing was that he and his team mates had won a Grand Final two years previously under the self-same circumstances of the 'right to challenge'.

Morris who was a police officer with the New South Wales force was destined to leave Western Suburbs and throw in his lot with the University club. It is strange that he did so as the club was amateur so perhaps his position in the police forced him to do so. On the other hand, we get a different perspective on the decision in the Referee on the 29th March 1933. The Cynic shows that there really is nothing new in the game and there was a type of salary cap even back in 1933 although it went by another name:-

"The Retention Committee to take practical steps to provide strength to weaker Sydney teams in order that they may be brought approximately to the playing standard of South Sydney, Eastern Suburbs and Western Suburbs."

This initiative was in the hands of Flegg, Miller and Rowland and perhaps Morris was persuaded to switch clubs in an attempt to strengthen the University playing squad. The Retention Committee was set up by the NSWRL to provide clubs with money to assist them in retaining players who would otherwise be lost to country rugby or to the northern state. Given that University was traditionally an amateur club we must assume that it was the Retention Committee that funded Morris. Was this a very early example of attempts to even up the competition between clubs in Sydney?

Not only that but they actually got Arthur Hennessy and the league Secretary Horrie Miller to coach the club as the new season approached! As Cynic writing in the Referee revealed:-

"Rugby League fans in Sydney have been much interested in the development of teamwork and tactics by the University as revealed in the trials. The team under the coaching guidance of Messrs Miller and Hennessy, for some weeks is responding well. Every Sunday they spend the forenoon at practice and after luncheon together return to the field to continue practice. This, they will continue throughout the season."

In yet another irony with regard to his career his first game for University in this 1933 season was played at Pratten Park on the first day of the season, the opponents were none other than Western Suburbs. When he had debuted for Wests way back the opposition that day had been University. On that occasion he had helped Wests to overcome the University side.

It did not take Morris long to show just what Wests had lost and University had gained as the reporter wrote of the first score in the game:-

"A brilliant movement by Uni. Ended in Morris scoring a fine try. McInerney passed to McKinnon to Ogg to Morris near the 25. Morris ran well, out pacing the opposition and brushing McMillan aside went over in the corner. McKinnon failed to convert. University 3-0."

Sadly, the University side could not consolidate and the game ended in a 32-22 defeat to Morris's former club. The Cynic following the game singled Morris out for praise:-

"R. Morris played a strong, rugged, fast game as University centre against his old Western Suburbs colleagues. They found him very difficult to tackle. On form at Pratten Park Morris has improved in a marked manner in the finer points of centre three-quarter back play. His football was so good that he looked a high grade state centre three-quarter, in fact a real Kangaroo."

However Cynic in the Referee seems to have kept a close eye on the work being done at the University and it appears both the team and Morris had benefitted greatly from the coaching:-

"The special attention given to strengthening the 'Varsity team in its personnel is also bearing fruits. The big Western Suburbs centre three-quarter R. Morris if trial form is a true guide is toning his attack with finer judgement. At times with Western Suburbs he was disposed to run too far with the ball. Now he is running far enough to create an opening and then by passing the ball, the game is opened up and he is able to reappear in the attack a pass or two later."

Cynic when assessing players worthy of selection for the upcoming State games felt that Dave Brown was the best centre he had seen play that season but Morris was at least as good as any of the others. He even went so far as to rate Morris as a centre in the same mould as the great English player James Lomas.

In that 1933 season in the inter-state games Morris really came to the fore and was looked upon as a certainty to make selection for the up-coming tour to England. It seemed he had the world at his feet for when he gained selection, he was just twenty-five and in the prime of his rugby league career. The selectors certainly had high hopes that at last they had produced a centre who was probably the best the game had witnessed in the last twenty years. More importantly it was felt that Morris was the player who could wrest the Ashes away from the English in the up-coming tour. It had been almost twelve years since that particular trophy had been in Australian hands.

When the tour party left Sydney aboard the Jervis Bay on the 4th July, Morris who had a great deal of experience in training systems from his police training approached the tour managers and was allowed to produce a series of exercises designed to keep the players as fit as was possible while on board ship. The players responded to his efforts with enthusiasm each morning. It was only when the ship set sail from Freemantle bound for Colombo in Ceylon now Sri Lanka that problems occurred. The players were engaged in sparring to keep fit. Morris was actually sparring with another player when he was accidentally struck a heavy blow on the ear.

The result of the blow was a burst ear-drum and resulted in him needing daily treatment in the ship's hospital. Sadly, the wound did not really respond well to the treatment and when the ship reached Colombo while Morris and the others were swimming in the pool on board ship the ear was to suffer a catastrophic infection. The ear that had been so troublesome became infected and once more treatment was necessary. He was placed in the ship's hospital for the ten days from Colombo to Malta. Try as they may the medical staff on board could not successfully treat the injury to his ear and his physical condition began to deteriorate.

His health continued to deteriorate as the ship passed through the Suez Canal into the Mediterranean and so serious did it become that the medial staff radioed ahead to arrange for Morris to be taken off the ship at Malta. The Navy arranged for Morris to be winched on to a Lighter from which he was taken into the harbour at Malta. He was quickly transferred to the Blue Sisters Hospital where he was put into the care of Doctor Vella. While in the hospital he underwent emergency surgery on his inner ear. Sadly, his condition continued to deteriorate to such an extent that Doctor Vella contacted the Admiralty in Malta.

An ear specialist who was present with the British Mediterranean fleet in Malta at the time was sent for but before he could arrive sadly Morris passed away. It is believed that he contracted meningitis from the water in the swimming pool on board ship and the doctors could not save him. Certainly, the doctors thought his symptoms would suggest meningitis. When he had been taken off the ship Sam Haron a member of the North

Sydney club and a good friend of Morris who was accompanying the tour party went with him to the hospital as the tour party sailed on. Haron was on a sight-seeing tour with a friend in Malta when news reached him that Morris's health had deteriorated. He rushed back to the hospital and was with him when he died. Morris passed away on the 10th August 1933. He was just twenty-five years old.

His body was embalmed and returned home to Sydney at the request of his parents where it lay in the Sydney Town Hall. His body came by train from Melbourne and was met at Central Station by his father and brother and the coffin was later taken to the Andrew's Funeral Chapel in Morris's beloved Ashfield. Once there the coffin was draped with the Australian flag along with Morris's green and gold blazer emblazoned on the breast pocket in gold were the words 1933-34. His family had also placed on the coffin a simple wreath. After a short family service at 5.00pm the Chapel was opened to the Sydney public.

They came in thousands to honour the sportsman and filed passed the coffin as it lay in the Town Hall. People in smart business attire mingled with tradesmen in their work clothes each paying their own tribute to Morris. It was the greatest funeral of a sportsman in Sydney since the tragic death of the boxer Les Darcy. The coffin was carried into Sydney Town Hall for the service by four players from the University club and four from the Western Suburbs outfit.

The Town Hall was packed to capacity and thousands who could not gain admission stood head bowed in silence outside the building. In his eulogy Canon Hilliard said:-

"Ray Morris left his mark on the generation in which he lived and has left behind him a fragrant and abiding memory. He had won for himself the admiration and respect of those who loved clean sport and bright Australian manhood, and the vast assembly which attends his funeral today, is the most eloquent tribute that can be expressed to the splendid and remarkable achievements of this loveable young man. He

wrote only a line or two on the page of life, but we thank God for his splendid example and fellowship."

The service complete, the procession left for Waverley Cemetery under leaden skies which suggested even nature was mourning the loss. It passed through throngs who lined the streets as his coffin was taken to the cemetery for burial. It seemed that his rugby league career was full of ironies while he was playing but then he suffered the greatest irony of all. With his passing the Australian Rugby League had lost a potentially great player and Morris's parents had lost a son. The really sad thing is that he was an absolute certainly to have won a Test place once he had reached England and the tour began. As it was sadly death robbed him of that honour and he was destined to become one of if not the saddest No Hit Wonders the Australian rugby league had produced in a generation. Sadly, we shall now never know if that is true or not.

POST SCRIPT

Ray Morris is buried at Waverley Cemetery.

Section 15, Row 24 Grave Number 6636

In yet another tragedy for the Morris family Ray's brother Ron sadly died in tragic circumstance on 29th July 1935. He had watched Wests play Souths at Pratten Park on the Saturday and while in bed suffered a suspected heart attack complicated by a recent bout of influenza. His mother was at the time seriously ill in Lewisham hospital and it was thought that he was worried also by this. Ron Morris was laid to rest beside his younger brother just twelve day short of two years to the day Ray had died. Ron was just twenty-eight years old!

CHAPTER TWELVE

MELVILLE JOSEPH GLASHEEN ESTATES TOWNSVILLE 1933

Back between the two World Wars the rugby world in Australia was a very narrow and parochial thing. New South Wales may well have relinquished control to some extent to The Australian Board of Control but that was only on paper. They dominated that Board and still ran the game as they thought fit. The northern State of Queensland was still at times very much kept in its place with regard to rugby league matters. It was in this atmosphere that players operated and in New South Wales the Sydney competition was king. While in Queensland to a lesser extent it was the leagues operating in the Bulimba Cup that ruled the roost.

Given such a situation it was very difficult if not nay on impossible for a player playing the game outside of these two spheres to gain any type of representative honours. There was one man who did break the mould but as we shall see he was very quickly put back into his place in the grand scheme of things. That player was Melville Glasheen who tended to go by the name of 'Mick'. He played his rugby in the far north of Queensland for the Estates club in Townsville.

Glasheen was actually born on the 26th September 1904 in the little gold mining town of Ravenswood. Ravenswood is around one hundred kilometres south of Townsville. He was the eldest of three brothers with Eddie and Ken they were a formidable trio. Ravenswood in 1904 was still a bustling place producing an abundance of gold although the boom years of the gold rush were behind it. Glasheen like many of his age was constantly looking for something to occupy his time. Sport was one outlet for all that youthful energy. When he went to senior school, he played rugby league and was a very powerful centre.

As he continued to grow, he slowly but surely gravitated toward the forwards. Leaving school, he continued his career in the Townsville Rugby League playing for the Estate club in 1920. Like many before him and after at first it was difficult to decide just what his best position was but once the club put him between two props that problem was solved. He proved to be a natural hooker and his ability was quickly recognized by the district selectors. It was obvious to all that he was a hooker who was well above the average in that position.

He was quickly to gain selection for the Townsville representative junior-minor team in that first year of 1920. He progressed to the Townsville Junior Grade representative outfit and from there he seemed never to look back. He went on to represent the Townsville senior grade side becoming a bedrock of the scrum for the rep side. While all of this was going on, he had completed his apprenticeship as a carpenter and set about earning a living. It was in 1929 that he first came to the attentions of selectors further afield that the far north Queensland. He was selected to play at hooker in a combined Townsville-Rockhampton side that played a New South Wales touring side.

Two years later he was in the North Queensland team that defeated South Queensland and his reputation was growing in the northern state. In 1932 he went down to Brisbane with the North Queensland team and played in the two games on that tour. His performances were such that the Queensland selectors awarded him his 'State Cap' when he was selected to play for his state. In that same year when the Englishmen visited Queensland in the June, he was in the North Queensland side that faced them. Strangely enough when the North Queensland team was announced Glasheen's name was followed by (Gargeth) which would suggest he had switched clubs! While all of this rep football was going on, he was still turning out regularly for his club.

The 1933 season however, was to prove to be the most momentous one in his career. At the start of the season he was selected to take part in a series of trial games with the intention of selecting a Queensland party that was to travel to Sydney to play New South Wales in the inter-state series. These games had added importance as they were to be used also as trial games for selection to tour England at the end of the season. In the final Queensland trial game, the selectors pulled a rabbit out of the hat.

They selected the whole Toowoomba club thirteen as one team the other team was a weakened state side. As was to be expected the very strong club side won the game but they did so without the majority of the ball. Glasheen had become what was for that period something of a rarity, namely a specialist hooker. In the game he out hooked his opposite number in the scrums with monotonous regularity. The selectors while selecting him for the tour party made the decision that in the first inter-state game in Sydney the Toowoomba side would represent Queensland. Glasheen was to be sidelined for the game it was a situation he was to experience more than once that year.

Seeing the error of their ways the Queensland selectors made changes and one thing that had stood out from the first encounter was that they had lost the scrums heavily. They did so again in the second encounter as a result Glasheen was drafted in for the third game. Whilst those first two games in the series were lost, the scrum count was heavily in favour of the northerners in the third game, Glasheen saw to that. The final and fourth game was to be played up in Brisbane and in keeping with former years following the game the selectors were to sit down and select the tour party for England.

When the states clashed this time, it was Queensland who came out winners by 10-8 and the win had its foundations laid by Glasheen. In both the games he had consistently out hooked first Little and then the international Fowell. On this occasion he won the first half scrums against Fowell 15-5 and repeated the dose in the second half with another 15-5 wipeout. As the players were at the reception following the game anxiously awaiting the deliberations of the selectors. Glasheen must have thought surely, he had done enough to gain selection.

When the selectors emerged and announced the squad to the waiting crowd, strangely they named three hookers in that squad, sadly Glasheen was not one of them. They had selected Bishop, Fowell and Little all three from the southern state. In actual fact the selectors had included a fourth hooker albeit an emergency rake in the form of Queensland forward Les Heidke. Heidke has actually played at hooker for Australia back in 1932. Glasheen took the decision in good stead and while others sympathized with him the authorities and the press were not so forgiving of the selectors. They had seen him out hook two of the three selected and thought his omission was a grave miscarriage of justice and wrote so. The North Queensland authorities were incensed and telegrammed their displeasure to the Queensland authorities:-

"Desire record North Queensland keen disappointment at Melville Glasheen's exclusion Australia touring side. In view of very favourable press reports and wonderful scrummage results in his favour we consider that our man was given a very raw deal. We will have more to say at the right time and the right place."

There is no doubt that the claims were probably true but at this time New South Wales authorities were a law unto themselves. In terms of the selection committee there were two representatives from each state but in the event of a deadlock then a third representative from the southern state was brought in to decide the issue. No New South Wales rep was going to go for a Queensland player at the expense of a New South Wales player! We were to see their heavy handed approach again before the tourists left for England.

Harry Sunderland a Queenslander himself and manager of the touring party did not have a vote in the selection of players but had his say on the matter in the Telegraph which was reproduced in the Townsville Daily Bulletin on the 20th June. He wrote:-

"The disappointment at the non-inclusion of the North Queensland hooker Melville (Mick) Glasheen must have been obvious to those who heard me speak over the radio. Glasheen has rarely been seen by the selectors who see so much of the other candidates. He has impressed me and others by his general demeanor and personality in training and team housing. In the two games he played against two separate hookers of New South Wales under two different referees and with different outside men in the loose head position and on two different grounds he had won the ball more decisively for Queensland than any other hooker we have had in years. His non-selection gives one the idea that the selectors have put him entirely out of court because he is not a shiner in any way in the open. Outside of Glasheen's non-selection the selectors cannot be heavily criticized."

There can be little doubt that the principle of a trial game is to select those players who perform the best on the day unless of course it is an Australian rugby league trial. Glasheen suffered simply because of where he played rather than on his ability and how he played. The selectors had not seen him play enough but was that their fault or Glasheens. If the harsh decision of the selectors in his regard was seen as just that, then a little later, they would make perhaps a couple of even more brutal decisions.

Having taken the decision on the chin Glasheen returned home to Townsville to simply get on with his life but fate was once again to play a part in his rugby career. On the Friday following the announcement of the party for England two of the player Norman and Bishop who had been carrying injuries went before the medical staff. The New South Wales authorities had ordered them to undergo a medical examination to determine if they were fit to go to England. Both players were declared by the doctors to be unfit for such a rigorous tour. Norman was replaced by a young Vic Hey while Bishop's replacement was 'Mick' Glasheen. In the north of Queensland justice was seen to have been done.

It is interesting to read an article by Harry Sunderland in the Telegraph up in Brisbane as it gives an insight into the odd selection protocols that seemed then as now to be in place with regard to representative selections. Sunderland had this to say in his report:-

"Thousands of supporters of the code thought that I possessed the casting vote and had decided against Glasheen. When it was really Charlie Russell of the Newtown Club of Sydney who had given his casting vote against Glasheen. Fowell comes from the Newtown club, Russell went to England from the Newtown club in 1911. Perhaps he had leaning for Fowell. Perhaps not!"

Nepotism comes in many forms and most certainly was not dead when it came to a New South Walian supporting one of their own! The article went on to give a good insight into Glasheens own reaction to his non-selection. While all the brouhaha was going on in Brisbane he was on the train back to Townsville and knew nothing of it. When asked of matters on his return home he told the reporter:-

"I suppose I can consider myself unlucky for after we had won on Saturday my friends kept telling me I had written my ticket for England. There were many New South Wales players besides all my Queensland friends who believed that I would be one of the chosen few and when the team was announced one of the first men to shake my hand and sympathise with me was Frank McMillan the New South

Wales captain. However, it is all over now. It was a case of many are called and few were chosen and I have forgotten all about it."

I suppose that statement was a measure of the man. It was Kipling who wrote if you can meet success and failure and treat them both the same you will be a man my son. Glasheen did just that.

The local Townsville paper carried an article which shows how the news of his re-inclusion into the tour party was greeted there and is worth seeing in detail:-

"The popularity of Melville ("Mick") Glasheen was very appropriately illustrated on Monday afternoon when some 200 friends and well-wishers crushed into the lounge of the Excelsior Hotel at the invitation of football administration to bid au revoir to him on the eve of his departure for Brisbane to join the other Queensland representatives, hence to Sydney to embark with the Kangaroos for the Rugby League tour to England...

It had all been a hurried up affair, but at the procession to be held at night Townsville residents would turn out in full force to do honour to him...

Mr A.W. Fadden L.M.A. then presented him with a travelling suitcase and an Australian made travelling rug on behalf of the football fraternity...

Prior to his departure Glasheen was enthusiastically farewelled at the Railway Station by a crowd of about 1500 people. At 7.15 a procession headed by the West End Boys Band moved from the Post Office with the popular Estates representative carried shoulder high by several of his club members."

The sent off was far from complete for when the train stopped at the Home Hill Station there were hundreds of people waiting on the platform to greet it or more precisely to greet Glasheen. The members of the local rugby league club were wanting to give him a good send off. After a number of speeches were made Glasheen was presented with a leather head guard on the inside of which had been inscribed "Good Luck".

One can gauge just how much his selection meant to the rugby fraternity in that far north Queensland rugby outpost. With his departure he became North Queensland's very first tour representative. Sadly, that was to be as good as it got for him. It is true that one players misfortune is another players opportunity and that was the case here. When he got to Sydney and just before the ship set sail, he was to receive yet another kick in the teeth from the selectors.

The Queensland forward Les Heidke had arrived in Sydney carrying an injury and there was some concern expressed by the New South Wales authorities. Heidke had been examined by medical staff up in Queensland and passed fit to go on tour. The Sydney based selectors were not happy with the decision of their northern counterparts. The tour party was actually photographed in their tour uniforms for publicity purposes and actually published in the newspapers when the decision was made to subject Heidke to another medical examination this time by doctors in Sydney. They for whatever reasons disagreed with their medical colleagues in Brisbane and declared the player was not fit to tour. It was a cruel and brutal decision to spring on a player so close to departure but does show the lack of feeling the southern authorities had for the northern state.

In the aftermath of this decision the selectors made another crass decision and their actions were a direct slur on Glasheen. There were already three hookers in the tour party, Fowell, Little and Glasheen but Heidke's replacement was to be the Queensland and Toowoomba veteran hooker Dan Dempsey who had toured the Old Country on the last tour in 1928. It was a decision that showed the confidence or lack thereof the selectors had in the far north Queensland hooker Glasheen. He must have realized the writing was on the wall for him even before the tour had begun. He was going to have to be twice as good as the other hookers even to gain selection and so it proved to be the case.

The tourist sailed out of Sydney and onto England and on the way they stopped at Colombo in Sri Lanka and there played an exhibition game, the first in the country. They repeated that when they stopped off in Egypt. It was not all pleasant however as they had left Ray Morris behind in Malta and then got the terrible news that he had succumbed to his illness and passed away. It was a terrible blow and affected the whole party but they simply had to get on with the job in hand. ***(See the earlier chapter that deals with the career of Ray Morris.)***

When the players arrived in England Glasheen along with a number of players were suffering from the flu it had dire consequences for him as he was out of action as the tour training began in earnest. As the tour began once again we witnessed the short sighted selection policy that seems to have been the norm on every tour to England at that time. As the 1911-12 tour had won the Ashes by the approach of Ford and Quinlan subsequent managers had adopted the same philosophy namely to win at any cost every game. In order to do that you played your strongest team at every opportunity. To do that you needed to decide just who were going to make up your strongest thirteen. The two managers on this tour seemed to have decided on a first thirteen and played them at every opportunity.

If Glasheen was not aware of his position in the hooking 'pecking order' before the party arrived, he was on the 23rd August. On that Wednesday afternoon the Australian and English teams played a 7-a-side game in Leeds the visitors were captained by Dan Dempsey the very late replacement. When the team for the first game of the tour was announced the hooking spot went to Fowell. If that were not bad enough four other players were instructed to take their gear in case of any unforeseen problems at St. Helens, one of the four was the hooker Dempsey. Claude Corbett writing in the Sun informed us that Glasheen had been bed ridden for over a week with bronchitis. The illness was to have consequences for him as we shall see.

The first ten games of the tour were all won and saw Fowell play five of them Dempsey four and Little one. The crazy thing is as Corbett revealed was that Little played only one game in the opening part of the tour as the selectors felt he was too small to compete with the English hookers! Surely that would have been known back in Australia when the tour party was being selected. Glasheen was still recovering from illness and on the 20th September Corbett reported he was getting better and would probably play the following week, he did not. As Glasheen had not yet played a game on the tour there was no chance what so ever that he would be considered for the first Test match.

It was not until the twenty eighth game of the tour against Rochdale Hornets on the 5th December that Glasheen was to pull on a shirt. Corbett wrote that it was his second game of the tour but this was obviously incorrect as he had not played a game up to that time with Dempsey, Little and Fowell being on duty in all the previous games. This after newspaper report after newspaper report mentioned the fact that English hookers were out hooking the Australian rakes. In total as far as research has been able to unearth, he was to play only one game on the tour and score one try not two are some newspapers reported.

It was not the best experience for Glasheen he had in the past out hooked all three of the other hookers in the party but was never given the opportunity to state a case for inclusion in a Test side. The bronchitis that had struck him down at the beginning of the tour most certainly had worked against him. All the other hookers in the party had consistently been out hooked by their opposite number but all had been given a decent run of games to see just what they could do, Glasheen was never afforded that luxury. He like others before him and certainly many after him had suffered the vagaries of selectors one eyed view of how a Test series in England could and should be won. It took them almost fifty years before they actually managed to do so.

Glasheen returned home a sadder and probably a wiser man. He returned to Townsville and continued his career with the Estates club. He was out of sight out of mind with regard to the international selectors and they never did call on him again preferring to go with New South Wales rakes. When he retired, he had a very successful coaching career in the far north Queensland rugby league scene. In 1946 he was to coach the Townsville representative side to victory over their Cairns rivals to take out the Carlton Shield.

He died 2nd September 1971 and is buried at Woongarra Crematorium in Townsville. He reached the heights but sadly did not get to the top of the mountain and so was destined to be a No-Hit Wonder.

CHAPTER THIRTEEN

MICK SHIELDS QUIRINDI 1935

Michael 'Mick' Shields arrived in the game of rugby league by a circuitous route and almost reached the very top in the game. He was born in 1912 not in Australia but in the coal mining town of Cowdenbeath in Scotland to Michael and Mary Shields. In 1915 when World War One was at its height some how the family managed to board a ship and set sail for Australia. We have no way of knowing just how the family was able to get on board a ship bound for Australia. The strange thing is that evidence would suggest that Michael senior worked in the coal mines in Cowdenbeath. At that time, he would have been in a 'reserved' occupation and it is difficult to understand how he was allowed not only to leave his occupation but get aboard a ship for the then very dangerous voyage down to Australia.

One explanation could be that the family arrived in Australia before that date. Research shows that a Shields family arrived in Sydney in 1913 a year after Micks birth. Mary is shown on the records as being head of the family which would suggest that Michael the father had travelled down to Australia ahead of his family.

The then three year old Mick arrived in the coal mining community of Kurri Kurri up in the Hunter Valley. We can assume that the father began working in the coal mines in the area swapping war torn Scotland for a more peaceful and quiet north New South Wales. Growing up and attending school Mick would have been introduced to the game of rugby league while at school and on completing his schooling he graduated to the Kurri Kurri junior club and progressed through the ranks eventually making his first grade debut as a hooker in 1933 aged twenty one.

Once in the first grade Shields quickly gained a reputation as a hooker of quality, one who could be relied upon to ensure his team had more than a fair share of the ball from the scrums. In addition, he also showed that he was more than useful with the ball in hand and also when the hard defensive work needed to be done. In that first season he developed into a hooker of great quality and began to attract the attention of the country representative selectors. However, with the season at an end the twenty one year old actually left Kurri Kurri and relocated to Quirindi.

The Maitland Mercury carried the news on the 9th March 1934 that Shields and George Brown had signed to play for Quirindi. Such was the popularity of both players that a large crowd gathered to see them off to pastures new. At the time Shields was unemployed so I suppose the offer of a contract to play for the new outfit would have been difficult to turn down. It is quite ironic that by moving to Quirindi which is around four hundred kilometres from Sydney while Kurri Kurri is only some 150 kilometres away he got on the radar of representative selectors. He was playing country football it is fair to say but playing it very well.

As the first season he spent at the new club came to an end such was his consistency in performance that he was one of the first to be approached by the committee to resign for the following season. Shields was happy to remain and the club were happy to secure his services for the 1935 season. As the new season came around it was to be a momentous one for Shields although he did not know it at the beginning.

He was more and more figuring in the thinking of the New South Wales country selectors who were well aware of his growing reputation as a rake who rarely lost the scrums in a game. His opportunity came towards the end of May when the county first and second teams to play Sydney were up for selection. The selectors could not justify selecting him for the first thirteen but put him in the scrum for the country second thirteen. The games were to be played in Sydney on Saturday the 25th May at the Cricket Ground.

As Shields took to the field it was in a steady downfall that had left the pitch in a treacherous state. The Sydney team had 'Chimpy' Busch and Ernie Norman in the halves and opposing Shields was the North Sydney hooker Fred Nolan. If the country boys were to have any chance, they needed to stifle the halves of Sydney and if possible keep the ball away from them at the scrums. They need not have worried as Shields provided his team with a steady stream of ball from the scrums and filled with such confidence his team mates simply tore into their opposite numbers when on defense. The country seconds walked off the paddock greatly pleased to have won the game 12-3. Shields performance and its effect of the result of the game had not been lost on the New South Wales selectors.

Following the game, they met to select the state team to oppose Queensland on the following Saturday. When they announced their deliberations as was expected a very strong team emerged with nine of them being Kangaroos. It was when they announced the reserves for the game that Shields saw that he was one of the reserve forwards for the game. The selectors then informed him that he was to remain in the city rather than return to Quirindi which augured well for him. The hooker for the state side was Percy Fairall the St George hooker.

Many were somewhat surprised by his selection but the respected Claude Corbett was not one of them. In a piece for the Sun on 29th May he made his feelings known:-

"The performance of Mick Shields the Quirindi hooker in the Sydney versus Country seconds match won him rapid recognition. Fred Nolan his opponent who played for North Sydney is looked upon as a fair example of a grade hooker but Shields hopelessly outpointed him last Saturday. Therefore, it is not surprising to find the Quirindi man amongst the New South Wales reserves against Queensland and it is quite on the cards that he will wear the sky blue jersey of the state before he returns to his country home."

How right Corbett turned out to be in his prediction for while in the stands for the first encounter on the second meeting he was on the paddock.

On Monday 3rd June when Shields took to the field, he was making his debut for New South Wales while his opposite number Dickson was doing the same for the maroons. Initially things did not go well for the sky blues as three penalties in the first ten minutes of the game put them behind 6-0. A little later with the home side attacking all came good for the hooker as Corbett said in the match report:-

"Queensland were penalized here, but Brown missed the goal. The Queenslanders were found badly lacking and Shields following fast, caught the ball on the bounce and scored before the northerners woke up to what was happening."

It could not get much better for the country boy to score for his state on debut by catching the opposition on the hop. It did his confidence no end of good and for the rest of the half he was in almost every forward attack for the sky blues. The other thing he was doing was what he always did he was winning the scrums hands down which allowed his team to constantly attack. The home side had fought back and as half time came, they were ahead 8-9 more importantly Shields had won the scrums by 17 to 7 as massive advantage for his side.

The second half followed a similar pattern and Shields was showing up well in the loose play. As the game ended the sky blue side were victorious by 18-14 and Shields had shaded the scrums in the second period 11-9. The selectors had seen enough they now felt they had two hookers of quality in Fairall and Shields. He was allowed to return home and was not called upon until the last game in the series. That fact was not lost on Claude Corbett who wrote in the Sun on the Wednesday following the game.

"Several men acquitted themselves admirably at their first inter state matches in Sydney in the two matches played between New South Wales and Queensland. Nobody could find fault with the two New South Wales hookers Percy Fairall and Mick Shields. Both of them served up a good share of the ball to their backs and played well in the open. There was a particularly fine piece of work by Shields on Monday when following up a kick from a penalty by Dave Brown he went after the ball, got it on the bounce and completely caught the Queenslanders napping to score the try."

It was the 6th July up in Brisbane before he pulled on the sky blue gernsey for a second time. He helped his side to a 23-9 victory and was quite pleased with his performance once again as were the selectors. What he did not know was the international selectors had been fully aware of the performance along with that of Percy Fairall. The big problem was that Shields was playing out in Quirindi way out west from Sydney. Fairall was playing week in and week out in Sydney so was constantly in the selector's minds. Still when the season was coming to its close the international selectors had to meet and decide on a squad to make a six match tour of New Zealand and the question was a simple one could a hooker playing country football cut it at international level.

The squad to make the six match tour to New Zealand was due to be released on the 28th August but the proverbial hit the fan when the names of the players were leaked and the newspapers published them on the Monday 27th. The two hookers named were as predicted Fairall and Shields the New South Wales rakes. It was obvious that the selectors even before the tour had begun had decided who was their first choice hooker and it was not Shields. A number of press reports emphasized the fact by referring to Shields as being the second hooker behind Fairall.

True to form when the players arrived in New Zealand for the first game Fairall was named in the hooking role. The game against Auckland was won 16-6 and for the game four days later down in Wellington Shields was named to start. The game was against the grandly titled New Zealand XIII in truth is was a team selected from Wellington, Hawke's Bay, Taranaki and Canterbury. In a high scoring match the Australians were victorious by a score of 47-31. The match report in the New Zealand Herald tells us the Australians won the ball from a great many scrums so Shields was playing true to form.

Two games played two hookers used and two wins all was set for the first Test on the Saturday and it was Fairall who got the jumper. Around 20,000 crammed into Carlaw Park to witness the first encounter between the two teams. To the surprise of everyone and the delight of the home team and its supporters it was New Zealand who took the game by a score of 22-14. Given the next game was to be the second Test Shields would have had high hopes of getting the hooking role, sadly that proved not to be the case.

When the team to play New Zealand was announced there were two changes McKinnon came into the centre to replace Mahon and Lewis replaced Gibbs in the second row. Shields was once again assigned to the stand. On this occasion the Australian team proved to be too strong for the hosts and won easily by 29-8. It was a better performance from the visitors and when Fairall crossed for a try in the corner and followed that up by scoring the last try of the game, Shields must have known his chance was gone. The series was tied at one game all and the selectors were certainly not going to risk the series by playing him in the deciding third Test match.

As was only to be expected the selectors named an unchanged side for the final Test just four days later and won the game going away by 31-8. In winning the series they also won the Courtney Goodwill Trophy which was a monster of a thing being at least four feet square and three feet tall. In the three important games of the short tour Shields had not figured and with the last game just four days hence it was he who took to the field not Fairall for the unimportant game. The game against Auckland was won easily 36-18 but it would have been small consolation for Shields.

When the players returned home, Shields went home to Quirindi true he had played for his country but not in a Test match. He surely knew that if he was to challenge Fairall not only for the Australian jersey but also the state jersey he needed to be playing in Sydney. The question was, would any club be willing to offer him a contract. When it became known he was looking to move it was the Western Suburbs club who stepped in with an offer. Shields was only too happy to join the club and set about preparing for the 1936 season with Wests.

He actually played in a trial game pre-season against Newtown and his old rival Fowell. In the first half following a kick to the head he suffered a badly cut eye. He refused to leave the fray knowing that if he could out hook Fowell it would auger well for his chances of ousting the hooker from the representative sides that coming season.

In the season opener on 13th April, 1936, Shields began his Sydney club career against Canterbury-Bankstown. There can be little doubt he was up for the challenge. Claude Corbett in his report on the game wrote:-

"Wests' forwards were working like Trojans, Shields being conspicuous."

For the first time in an age Shields was not winning the scrums but his play in the loose was more than making up for that. Sadly, however his debut game was lost 11-6 and he was badly beaten in the scrums also. In the second round it got worse as North Sydney beat Wests easily 28–8. In the third round the Wests team met Balmain and ran out winners 30-13 to register the first success for Shields. He would have thought that all was once again back on track with regard to his ambition sadly that was to prove not to be the case.

In round four following a 17-17 draw against Eastern Suburbs the Sydney versus Country teams were announced and once again Fairall got the first team spot and Shields once again had to be satisfied with the second team spot. It was Fairall who got the New South Wales jersey the following Saturday against Queensland and Shields was again sitting the game out. The pill would have got even more bitter the following Saturday when Sydney opened the England tour against the visitors with Fairall again in the hooking gernsey. He would retain it the following weekend when New South Wales faced England. It really was a case of it being harder to get dropped from an Australian representative side that to get selected.

While all of this was happening, Shields was having even more problems as following the fourth round game he had picked up a knee injury which at first seemed to be quite innocuous but proved to anything but. The knee did not respond to treatment and sadly Shields Sydney career was over after just four games. It was decided the knee would not stand up to the rigors of football at the highest level. He left the Wests outfit and moved north playing for the South Newcastle club where he stayed for two seasons before retiring from the playing side of the game. He was just twenty six years old.

Even thenit seems he fell foul of the residential rules in existence at the time. He had moved from Kurri-Kurri to Newcastle and all in rugby league circles felt he would turn out for the East Newcastle club. However, he actually moved into the South Newcastle club boundaries and lived there in December 1936 and January 1937. He actually played his first game for South Newcastle on the 10th April 1937. However, the league instructed him to obtain statutory declarations from a number of people to the effect that he was not living in Kurri-Kurri between December 1936 and January 1937. It appears authorities were just as pedantic with certain issues back then as they are today. The following season he was actually appointed as coach of the South Newcastle outfit.

All through the 1940s he was involved in development programmes for the game along with coaching. He spent a couple of seasons coaching the Cessnock club along with the Belmont club (Now the Lakes United club.). We know that in 1942 he was a member of the Cessnock club's committee and offered to play for the club once again if the rule forbidding committee members from actually playing could be rescinded. In 1951 he joined Cessnock radio station 2CK where he hosted a weekly rugby league programme. In 1972 at the age of sixty he retired from his job as an engineer in the coal mining industry. Shields passed away in 1983 at the age of seventy one.

In 2010 the Kurri Kurri club were selecting their team of the century. They had not forgotten the first ever player from the club to gain international recognition. They named him as hooker in that team. There is little doubt that his career in the game had seen a meteoric rise from country football with Kurri Kurri to the green and gold on the national side in New Zealand. Equally due to injury his demise was as rapid. The knee injury robbed him of the chance of earning that elusive Test spot for Australia. There is no doubt had he remained injury free he would by playing in Sydney been seem regularly by representative selectors and put pressure on Fairall. As it was, he was destined by injury to become yet another one of those players deemed to be a No-Hit-Wonder.

CHAPTER FOURTEEN

GORDON DOUGLAS MacLENNAN NEWTOWN/COOMA 1937

MacLennan is the player 2nd from the right in the middle row.

When the Secretary of the club approached MacLennan early in the 1937 season it was with an offer he was to find difficult to turn down. The Cooma club in the Snowy Mountains were looking for a captain/coach and thought he was the man for the job. The problem was that he had been working on the wharfs all of his life since finishing school. The other thing was that the only rugby he had played at the top level had been for the Newtown 'Bluebags'. Now he was being asked to leave both, up sticks and move some one hundred and fifty kilometres or so away from the city.

To add to his problem, with the season in progress at the end of it was the carrot of the tour to England by the green and gold. Not that he felt he had much chance in securing a place on that tour. The competition for places from other prop forwards in the game was fierce. Almost every club had props worthy of such an honour. After deliberation and a chat with the Newtown committee he took the decision to take up the Cooma offer and moved away from Sydney.

It turned out to be the best move he could have ever made. With his move he came on the radar of the representative selectors not for the city but for the country. The big strong ex-wharfie was ideally built for the rough and tumble of the front row that was even more rugged in the country than in Sydney. To his delight he was soon to be back on his way to the big city this time to represent the country XIII who were to meet the city XIII on the 29th May 1937. It was to bring him to the view of selectors for the New South Wales team for the first time really. He was to play in the second row on that Saturday afternoon at the Cricket Ground.

There were around twenty five thousand in the ground to witness this first representative game of the season. The game would have held no fears for MacLennan as he was opposed by players he had played against for the last three seasons or so. The country forwards were having the best of the encounter and on one occasion Prigg dummied through and passed to MacLennan with the line at his mercy sadly he could not hold the pass. Later he was involved in a great passing movement but his final pass went astray and another scoring chance was lost. Come half time it was country who were ahead but only by a point at 5-4.

McLennan was doing more than enough both in attack and defense to impress those watching and the second half proved to be more of the same from him. The country pack out played their opponents and MacLennan was always in the thick of the action. As he and his team mates left the paddock at the end of the game, they had won 20-12 much to the surprise of many pundits. He had little aspirations following the game knowing that one good performance was not going to be enough to impress any selector, how wrong he was.

What happened is best described by Claude Corbett writing in the Sunday Sun following the game under the headline:-

"Sudden rise to fame of country star MacLennan"

"Sudden and unexpected rises to fame are often associated with selection to representative football teams. Gordon MacLennan formerly of Newtown now of Cooma comes into that category.

After he had played for Newtown against Balmain on April 26th MacLennan probably said goodbye to all hopes of state representation this season, at least. But forces were at work unknown to him, in his favour.

Without seeing him play Southern Selectors included him in the team to meet Western at Wollongong last Sunday.

Then MacLennan came to Sydney, was in that great game yesterday for country, and will now wear the sky blue of NSW for the first time against Queensland next Saturday.

Prior to yesterday MacLennan's highest honours had been had been for Sydney seconds against country seconds last season."

It seems that he had done more than enough to impress the selectors and had made the state side for the very first time and this after leaving Newtown.

On the Saturday the ground was a bit of a quagmire and the game turned into a something of an arm wrestle. MacLennan played well and early in the second half while supporting an attack by the three quarters he was on hand to take a low pass to him from his wingman Tottey collect and dive over for a score. The home side won the game by a score of 21-9. The match while important had added significance owing to the upcoming tour to England. MacLennan must have felt he had done his chances little harm with his efforts that afternoon.

His optimism would have, he must have felt been misplaced when the selectors announced four changes to the side for the clash the following Saturday. Corbett writing in the Sunday Sun felt the changes were not due to poor performances but rather the international selectors avowed intention of giving as many players as possible the opportunity of impressing them. MacLennan would not have seen it that way I feel sure. Corbett was sure that the Cooma player was in the category of having done enough to impress the selectors.

It had been a hectic couple of weeks for MacLennan and it had seen him reach heights perhaps he never felt he would achieve and it was a far cry from the past four seasons or so. Having spent all his working life on the wharf in Sydney he had developed into a big strong young man ideal for the sport of rugby league. He had come into the world on 23rd November 1914 just as the world was slowly coming to grips with the war which was to alter it forever.

Given the rules that existed at that time when he began to play the game, he was to play for the Newtown junior club in the President's Cup competition and graduated to the Bluebags as a twenty year old with a fearsome reputation in the junior game. He made his first grade debut on 16th June 1934 in round seven. The opponents were Eastern Suburbs and he was on the losing side that afternoon going down 23-9. In that first season with the club he went on to play seven games.

The next season he was an almost ever present turning out sixteen times in what was a mixed season for the club with eight wins and eight defeats. The 1936 season seemed to follow a similar path he played fourteen games but managed to be on the winning side just seven times. True he had gained selection for the Sydney second team to play country seconds but nothing had come from that representative debut. He would have felt he was perhaps at a cross road in his rugby career. He was just twenty two years old playing in the Sydney competition but there were players who had a few more years of experience under their belts than he had. It was they who seemed to be attracting the attention of representative selectors.

The question was, did he want to carry on playing with Newtown and hope that the club fortunes would turn around. He like every other player knew very well it was the successful clubs that supplied the majority of players to the state and national sides. As the 1937 season began MacLennan was once again plying his trade in the second row. The first game saw Newtown go down to Eastern Suburbs and the next two games were won but MacLennan had been approached by officials from the Cooma club to become the captain/coach. It had been a difficult decision at the age of twenty three did he turn his back on the Sydney competition for bush country football. As we now know he made the decision to move down to the Snowy Mountains and the Cooma club.

Now here he was just a few short weeks after leaving Sydney back and a state representative at that, but a state player who had been dropped after just one game. Just three weeks later the final inter-state game was played up in Brisbane after which the team to tour England would be selected and announced to the press. MacLennan was not in Brisbane when the squad was announced and twenty two New South Wales players were in the party and just six from Queensland. There was no one more surprised than him when he was told he was in the squad to travel back to England with the green and gold.

When Corbett managed to contact him when the squad had been announced on the Saturday evening he told him:-

"When I was dropped from the second New South Wales team I thought my chance had gone. I really didn't expect selection. Eric Lewis is a great forward, it is great news."

As the tour party prepared to leave for England the Newtown club arranged a farewell send-off for their former player as did the Cooma club who now had their first international player. The tour was to begin over in New Zealand where two Test matches were to be played along with a game against a New Zealand Maori team. It was the 11th August when MacLennan ran out to play against the Maori side having not figured in the Test game four days earlier. The home side won the game 16-5. For MacLennan it was a sign of things to come.

The tour party must surely have known that they were sailing toward a Europe once again torn by war, this time it was a civil war in Spain. More alarmingly was the news that was filtering through that the German Luftwaffe at the expressed command of Adolph Hitler were throwing their weight behind the forces of General Franco. What no one knew then was the German airmen were perfecting tactics they would put into brutal operation just a couple of years later when the whole of Europe was once again engulfed in war. It was quite ironic that MacLennan was born as World War One was beginning and was sailing to England as the seeds of World War Two were sprouting!

Once in England MacLennan did not have to wait long to see action as he was selected for the second game of the tour on 22nd September against York and he acquitted himself well in a 15-6 win. In his next outing he faced Wakefield Trinity and once again gave a good performance in a 17-10 win. The problem was that hoary old chestnut associated with Australian tour managers who decide what their best team is and are not prepared to alter it no matter how well other players performed.

We saw this yet again in the first Test played at Leeds. The Australians were by far the better side throughout the match but failed to win. They had only themselves to blame for a 5-4 loss. They made opening after opening only to hold onto the ball too long and get tackled or take the wrong option. The problem with a glorious defeat is that selectors tend to stick with the same players as they feel it will come right in the next Test. Following the Test in the mid-week game at Rochdale MacLennan turned out for his third game. It was not a great performance from the visitors but MacLennan did cross for a try in a 13-13 drawn match. He was once again selected for the mid-week encounter with Bradford which again saw him on the winning side. However, a pattern was developing in that he seemed to figure in the 'lesser' games but not in the more important ones.

In his fifth game against Warrington MacLennan seems to have put himself about quite a bit. Warrington had the former Australian skipper Dave Brown in the centre and he led his team to an 8-6 win over the visitors. It seems from match reports that MacLennan not only managed to get on the wrong side of the referee but also the crowd. When he was cautioned the crowd were screaming 'Send him off.' Unfortunately, the crowd got their wish late in the game when he tackled Belshaw the full back after he had kicked the ball. So late was it the referee ordered him from the field. It was not the action the two managers would have been happy with.

As the tour progressed when the Test matches came around it was time for MacLennan to warm a seat in the stand while others took to the field. It total, he would pull on a green and gold shirt some sixteen times but sadly never in a Test match. With the tour over and on his return, he went back down to Cooma and continued playing. Sadly, events in Europe were taking a turn for the worse as Hitler continued with his demands and led the world headlong into yet another conflict.

During the war years MacLennan was to play the odd game for his old club Newtown and was finally to have some success. It came in the biggest game of the season in 1943 when Newtown met North Sydney in the Grand Final. He was in the team playing prop forward on one side of the scrum while the other side was held up by the great Frank 'Bumper' Farrell. Over sixty thousand supporters crammed into the Cricket Ground a record for a club match up to that time. People were arriving at the ground at around 8.30am. yet the turn stiles were not opening until 10.00am.

As the ground filled up people tried to climb over the wall, climb trees and poles to get a glimpse of the upcoming game. One bright spark even picked the lock on one of the gates leading into the ground and a couple of hundred spectators rushed into the ground before the police could close the gate again. It was as if every rugby league supporter in the city wanted to watch the encounter between the two rivals. In the end it proved to be no contest as Newtown ran away with the game winning 34-7 and MacLennan now had a Premiership win under his belt.

He then seemed to drift out of the game as he entered his thirties and returned to his old job working on the wharf in Sydney had he ever left it. He had reached almost to the very top in the game, while an Australian tourist he was destined not to become a Kangaroo. The war curtailed his and many others careers so we shall never know if he would have gone on to gain that elusive Test jumper. He was after all only twenty four years old on his return from England. He was though to become yet another No-Hit-Wonder in this great game of rugby league.

EPILOGUE

There are a great many more players who were to suffer the same fate as the fourteen whose careers are chronicled albeit briefly in this book. They also we are sure would have great stories to tell either in the exploits on the field or equally as interestingly off it. Hopefully at some stage their stories will once again be returned to the public gaze as it were. For now, they are destined to remain simply names on a list of players who are Australian rugby league players.

Below is a list of all pre war players who were to become No-Hit Wonders of the game along with their heritage number

34	Dobbs, Alf 'Bullock	1908	Balmain	0
36	Bailey, Bill	1908	Newcastle	0
38	Moir, Peter	1908	Glebe	0
50	Neill, William 'Webby'	1909	South Sydney	0
51	Stuntz, Johnno	1909	Eastern Suburbs (Sydney)	0
52	Brown, Dave	1909	Eastern Suburbs (Sydney)	0
53	Carpenter, Stan	1909	Newcastle	0
54	Bollard, Arthur	1909	North Sydney	0
56	O'Brien, Arthur	1909	Fortitude Valley	0
57	Patfield, Ernie	1909	Newcastle	0
59	Charles Ross	1909		0
60	Harvey, Arch	1909	Bundaberg	0
62	Fenelley, Sid	1909		0
72	Burge, Peter	1911	Glebe	0
73	Darmody, Steve	1911	South Sydney	0

78	Gillett, George	1911	?, NZ	0
81	McMurtrie, Charlie	1911	Balmain	0
82	Murray, Joe	1911	Newtown	0
83	Savory, Charlie	1911	Ponsonby Ponies	0
84	Stuart, Bob	1911	Annandale	0
86	Woodward, Frank	1911	?, NZ	0
110	Kerwick, John	1919	South Sydney	0
120	Laing, Bert	1921	City Rovers (Auckland)	0
121	Norman, Rex	1921	Eastern Suburbs (Sydney)	0
122	Peters, Herman	1921	North Sydney	0
124	McGrath, Eddie	1921	South Sydney	0
125	Brown, Edwin	1921	Newtown (Toowoomba)	0
153	Henderson, Arthur	1929	Booval	0
157	Finch, Harry	1929	South Sydney	0
158	Holmes, Jack	1929	Newtown	0
161	Root, Eddie	1929	South Sydney	0
162	Upton, Jack	1929	Souths (Toowoomba)	0
163	Kadwell, Harry	1929	South Sydney	0
166	Sellars, Les	1929	Starlights (Ipswich)	0
177	Denny, Henry	1933	Western Suburbs (Brisbane)	0
178	Doonar, Frank	1933	Rialto (Ipswich)	0
190	Glasheen, Melville	1933	Estates (Townsville)	0
197	Bichel, Henry	1935	East Ipswich	0
198	Collins, Edward	1935	Norths (Brisbane)	0
201	Shields, Mick	1935	Quirindi	0
202	Whittle, Gordon	1935	(Toowoomba)	0
210	Griffiths, Frank	1937	Balmain	0
211	McLennan, Gordon	1937	Newtown	0
213	Robison, Harry	1937	Toowoomba	0
214	Thompson, Roy	1937	North Sydney	0

Printed in Great
Britain
by Amazon

31616887R00092